USING
THEOLOGICAL
BOOKS
AND
LIBRARIES

PRENTICE-HALL INTERNATIONAL, INC., *London*
PRENTICE-HALL OF AUSTRALIA, PTY., LTD., *Sydney*
PRENTICE-HALL OF CANADA, LTD., *Toronto*
PRENTICE-HALL FRANCE, S.A.R.L., *Paris*
PRENTICE-HALL OF JAPAN, INC., *Tokyo*
PRENTICE-HALL DE MEXICO, S.A., *Mexico City*

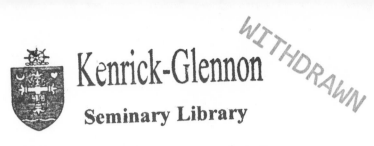
USING THEOLOGICAL BOOKS AND LIBRARIES

ELLA V. ALDRICH
Author of *Using Books and Libraries*

THOMAS EDWARD CAMP
Librarian, The School of Theology
The University of the South

Illustrated by John Chase

Prentice-Hall, Inc.
Englewood Cliffs, N. J.

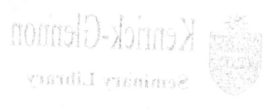

Library of Congress Catalog Card No.:
63–13298

Printed in the United States of America
C

FOREWORD

The need for this manual seemed to be apparent. Consultation with many of the clergy, with theological school faculty, and with theological librarians confirmed our conviction. It can be helpful especially to beginning seminarians, and upperclassmen will find it useful. Few in either group are skilled in the use of a library and its tools, nor are they generally familiar with a wide variety of reference books. In addition, this text can supplement a course in Research Methods.

Quality education on the graduate level is deeply involved with research, and the competence of the product is largely dependent upon the students' ability to use research sources with skill, wisdom, and facility.

Obviously, such a manual can cover only a bird's-eye view of research materials, but knowing how to use other sources will be the natural result of mastering the ones included here. Many theological libraries are understaffed with professional librarians, whose time for assisting students is limited. *Using Theological Books and Libraries* can equip students to do much research without the assistance of a librarian.

Work in preparing the manuscript was done in a number of theological school libraries in different sections of the country. The authors were advised and aided by some of the librarians and by other specialists. We are grateful to Miss Lucile Morsch, Deputy Chief Assistant Librarian, The Library of Congress; Robert F. Beach, Librarian, Union

Theological Seminary, New York City; The Rev. W. Patrick Donnelly, S.J., former President of Loyola University, New Orleans, Louisiana; The Rev. Edward B. Rooney, S.J., and The Rev. Paul A. Fitz-Gerald, S.J., Jesuit Educational Association; The Rev. James J. Kortendick, S.J., Head, and Dom Bernard Theall, O.S.B., Professor of Reference, Department of Library Science, Catholic University of America, Washington, D. C.; The Rev. Edmond F. X. Ivers, S.J., Librarian, St. Peter's College, Jersey City, N. J.; and The Rev. David Collins, Chaplain, The University of the South, Sewanee, Tennessee.

We are further grateful to John Chase, Editorial Cartoonist of the New Orleans *States*, for permission to use his illustrations from *Using Books and Libraries*; to the American Theological Library Association, for their permission to reprint material from their publication, the *Index to Religious Periodical Literature*; to the Catholic Library Association, for their permission to reprint items from the *Catholic Periodical Index*; and to The New York Times Company, for their permission to reprint two items from *The New York Times Index*.

E. V. A.

T. E. C.

CONTENTS

THEOLOGICAL LIBRARIES 1

CLASSIFICATION AND ARRANGEMENT OF BOOKS 2

THE CARD CATALOG 8

REFERENCE BOOKS 18

INDEXES: THEOLOGICAL PERIODICAL INDEXES,
GENERAL PERIODICAL INDEXES, OTHER INDEXES 23

THEOLOGICAL ABSTRACTING TOOLS 37

BIBLIOGRAPHIES 39

DICTIONARIES: THEOLOGICAL, GENERAL 47

ENCYCLOPEDIAS: THEOLOGICAL, GENERAL 52

YEARBOOKS, HANDBOOKS, DIRECTORIES 59

THE BIBLE: VERSIONS, COMMENTARIES,
CONCORDANCES, DICTIONARIES, ATLASES 67

BIOGRAPHY: THEOLOGICAL, GENERAL 77

RELIGIOUS HISTORY, GENERAL HISTORY, ATLASES 83

LITERATURE: THEOLOGICAL, GENERAL 92

PHILOSOPHY, PSYCHOLOGY, SOCIOLOGY, EDUCATION 97

MAKING A BIBLIOGRAPHY 100

INDEX 111

vii

THEOLOGICAL
LIBRARIES

An old story of library regulations at Brown University tells us that students came to the library four at a time when sent for by the librarian and were not allowed to go beyond the librarian's table on penalty of threepence for each offense!

The library of an institution of higher learning today is not the sheltered, awe-inspiring place it was twenty-five or thirty years ago. It is the hub of a wheel whose spokes reach into every department of the institution. No educational institution can develop or produce effective work without a strong library as its center; the stature of the library plays a major role in the academic rating of a university or of a college. This principle applies to schools in special fields and to a whole university.

Educational methods have changed and broadened so that both faculty and students are dependent upon the library. A knowledge of the use of the library is essential, not only to get the most out of the whole educational experience, but to save precious time.

No person of normal intelligence would attempt to pilot a plane or to swim in deep water without knowing how. The best way to learn any skill, and certainly an educational skill, is through instruction and practice, through which you learn how to find information quickly and easily in a library, for instance. The ideal is having a course in theological bibliography, which several theological schools have, just as law schools have a course in legal bibliography; but until all theological schools initiate such a course, an intelligent graduate student can help to equip himself through the use of a manual of instruction, which shows the use of library tools.

The average beginning seminarian has had some library experience, but his first trip to the theological library may be bewildering. This frequently happens in using a library of subject specialty. His two best tools are the library handbook and a manual of instruction in the use of theological books and libraries.

1

CLASSIFICATION
AND ARRANGEMENT
OF BOOKS

Classification

Since it is convenient and important to keep together all books on a subject, libraries have a device that makes such grouping possible. It is a classification system that groups books according to *subject*, thereby bringing together on the shelves all books on a given subject, such as Bible, or Christian Church, or Doctrinal Theology. There are many systems of classifying books, but the two most generally found in libraries are the Dewey Decimal Classification and the Library of Congress Classification. The latter uses the letters of the alphabet to classify books, for instance, BL is for *Religions. Mythology. Free Thought:* BL550–635 covers the subject *Worship.* The most commonly used system, however, is the Dewey Decimal, which assigns a *number* to each book. For example, 262.11 stands for Apostolic Succession, and all books on that subject will have that number and stand together on the library shelves.

The Union Theological Seminary in New York has developed still another classification system for special libraries in the field of Theology, and it is becoming widely used by those libraries. The system uses the letters of the alphabet, expanded with numbers; but it is different from the Library of Congress system. As an example, UG–UU cover Church Worship.

2

DEWEY DECIMAL CLASSIFICATION

Dewey divides all knowledge into nine major classes, with an extra class for works so general as to make a definite place in any of the nine classes impossible:

000 GENERAL WORKS
   010 Bibliography
   020 Library economy
   030 General cyclopedias
   040 General collected essays
   050 General periodicals
   060 General societies. Museums
   070 Journalism. Newspapers
   080 Polygraphy. Special libraries
   090 Book rarities

100 PHILOSOPHY
   110 Metaphysics
   120 Special metaphysical topics
   130 Mind and body
   140 Philosophic systems and doctrines
   150 Psychology
   160 Logic
   170 Ethics
   180 Ancient philosophers
   190 Modern philosophers

200 RELIGION
   210 Natural theology
   220 Bible
   230 Doctrinal. Dogmatics. Theology
   240 Devotional. Practical
   250 Homiletic. Pastoral. Parochial
   260 Church: institutions and work
   270 General history of the church
   280 Christian churches and sects
   290 Nonchristian

300 SOCIAL SCIENCES. SOCIOLOGY
   310 Statistics
   320 Political science
   330 Economics. Political economy
   340 Law
   350 Administration
   360 Associations and institutions
   370 Education
   380 Commerce. Communication
   390 Customs. Costumes. Folklore

400 PHILOLOGY
   410 Comparative

   420 English. Anglo-Saxon
   430 German and other Teutonic
   440 French. Provençal
   450 Italian. Rumanian
   460 Spanish. Portuguese
   470 Latin and other Italic
   480 Greek and other Hellenic
   490 Other languages

500 PURE SCIENCE
   510 Mathematics
   520 Astronomy
   530 Physics
   540 Chemistry
   550 Geology
   560 Paleontology
   570 Biology. Anthropology
   580 Botany
   590 Zoology

600 USEFUL ARTS
   610 Medicine
   620 Engineering
   630 Agriculture
   640 Home economics
   650 Communication. Business
   660 Chemic technology
   670 Manufactures
   680 Mechanic trades
   690 Building

700 FINE ARTS, RECREATION
   710 Landscape gardening
   720 Architecture
   730 Sculpture
   740 Drawing. Decoration. Design
   750 Painting
   760 Engraving
   770 Photography
   780 Music
   790 Amusements

800 LITERATURE
   810 American
   820 English. Anglo-Saxon
   830 German and other Teutonic

840 French. Provençal	930 Ancient history	
850 Italian. Rumanian	940	Europe
860 Spanish. Portuguese	950	Asia
870 Latin and other Italic	960	Africa
880 Greek and other Hellenic	970 Modern	North America
890 Other literatures	980	South America
900 HISTORY	990	Oceania and polar regions
910 Geography. Travels		
920 Biography		

Each major class is divided into ten smaller classes, each of which includes ten still smaller classes for further subdivisions of the main subject. Decimal expansion then makes it possible to provide a place for the smallest topic, as shown under 262.1 through 262.2 below:

200 RELIGION
210 Natural theology
220 Bible
230 Doctrinal theology
240 Devotional & practical
250 Pastoral theology
260 Christian church
261 Christian social theology
262 Church government and organization
   .1   Governing leaders
   .11 Apostolic succession
   .12 Episcopacy
   .13 Papacy
   .131 Papal infallibility
   .132 Temporal power of the pope
   .135 Election of the pope
   .136 Curia Romana
   .14 Clergy
   .2   Parish
270 Christian church history
280 Christian churches & sects
290 Other religions

Call Numbers

Having a number of books on the same subject, and therefore with the same class number, makes it necessary to distinguish among them in some way. This is done by combining a "book number" with the class number to make up the "call number" of the book—the number by which you call for a book at the Loan Desk and by which it is located on the shelf. If you are working in an open-stack library, you go directly to the shelf. The *book number* is composed of the first letter or two in the author's last name plus a number from the Cutter table of author numbers. Very often the first letter in the title of the book is then added. For instance, Henry Joel Cadbury's number is C121. He wrote *Jesus: What Manner of Man*, whose class number is 232.9; and the combination of the *class number* and the *book number* is the *call number* of the book, $\frac{232.9}{C121j}$. The letter *j* in the book number distinguishes this book from the author's *The Peril of Modernizing Jesus*, whose call number is $\frac{232.9}{C121p}$.

This system makes it impossible for two books to have the same combination of numbers. The call number appears on the book and in the upper left corner of every card for that book in the card catalog.

Arrangement

The arrangement of books on the shelves reads from left to right on each shelf and from top to bottom of the stack (section or group of shelves). The call numbers are read numerically, and decimals are valued just as in mathematics.

Library of Congress Classification

The Library of Congress Classification is used in many libraries whose collections are of considerable size, and it is becoming popular with university, state, and federal libraries. However, if a library collection has grown to great size using the Dewey Decimal Classification, it would be prohibitively expensive to change over to the Library of Congress Classification.

This classification utilizes the letters of the alphabet combined with Arabic numerals to classify library materials. A brief summary follows:

LIBRARY OF CONGRESS CLASSIFICATION

A	General Works. Polygraphy	N	Fine Arts
B	Philosophy. Religion	P	Language and Literature
C	History—Auxiliary sciences	PN	Literary History and Literature
D	History and Topography	Q	Science
	(except America)	R	Medicine
E-F	America	S	Agriculture, Plant and Animal
G	Geography. Anthropology. Sports		Industry
H	Social Sciences	T	Technology
J	Political Science	U	Military Science
K	Law	V	Naval Science
L	Education	Z	Bibliography
M	Music		

The expansion of BL is shown below:

BL RELIGIONS. MYTHOLOGY. FREE THOUGHT.

1–635	Religion in general
175–290	Natural theology
239–265	Religion and science
303–325	Mythology
350–390	Classification of religions
410	Relations of religions to one another
420	Relations of religion to science, art, ethics, etc.
425–547	Religious doctrines in general
550–635	Worship. Cultus
660–2630	History and principles
800–820	Classical
830–875	Germanic and Norse
800–980	Other European

UNION THEOLOGICAL SEMINARY CLASSIFICATION

AA–AZ	General Works
BA–BZ	Philology and Literature
CB–FY	Bible
GA–GW	Christian Literature, Patristics
HA–HZ	History
IJK	Church History, General, More than One Country

LA–MX	History by Country, Both Church History and Political History
N	Missions, General and Comprehensive Works. Theory of Missions
OA–OZ	Comparative Religion
PA–PZ	Sciences, Mathematics
QA–QZ	Philosophy
R	Systematic Christian Theology
SA–SZ	Sociology
TA–TZ	Education
UA	The Church, Its Constitution, Orders and Ministry
UB–UF	Church Law
UG–UU	Church Worship
V	Music, Hymnology
WA–WW	Practical Church Work
XA–XW	Care and Culture of the Individual Religious and Moral Life, Devotional Literature
Y	Fine Arts, Practical Arts, Medicine
Z	Reserved for Polygraphy and Miscellaneous Special Collections

The above classification system uses all of the letters of the alphabet combined with Arabic numerals to classify library materials dealing with religion and related subjects, whereas the Library of Congress Classification uses only BL through BX in classifying religious publications. Following is a brief expansion of Union Theological's letter *U*:

UA   THE CHURCH, ITS CONSTITUTION, ORDERS AND MINISTRY
   CHURCH LAW

UB–UB39	General, Historical and Oriental treatises
UB40–98	Western and Catholic church law
UC	Protestant church law
UD–UE	Church and state, ecclesiastical law by country
UF	Topics in comparative church law

   CHURCH WORSHIP

UG	The sacraments, baptism, Lord's supper, sacramentalia, minor devotional practices and church seasons
UH–UK	Liturgical worship, Eastern rites
UL–UN	Latin rite
UP–UU	Protestant liturgies, prayer

As an example of a comparison of the three systems, *The Cairo Geniza* is classified in Dewey as 221.44; in the Library of Congress as BS718; and in Union Theological as DF.

THE
CARD
CATALOG

Some students are unfamiliar with a card catalog because during their college or university experience they may have avoided any extensive use of the library or may have been victims of faulty or insufficient guidance in library use.

Many libraries still have their collections in closed stacks where only faculty and graduate students are allowed to work. The only key to such a collection is the card catalog. The present trend, however, in libraries of recent construction is *open* stacks where each person, faculty or student, goes for his books; everyone has direct access to the books, magazines and newspapers, pamphlets, and so on. Numerous theological libraries have followed the latter policy for some time, as have special libraries in other subject fields.

Even with such an arrangement, you are still dependent upon the card catalog to find out what the library has, where to find it, and how to locate it. This becomes even more significant in larger libraries, since by their very nature books deal with far more than one subject and cannot be classified in each subject field. Wandering around among thousands of books looking for the ones you need or want isn't intelligent!

Index to the Book Collection

The card catalog is an alphabetical index to the books in the library. It is a guide to the book collection just as an index in a book is a guide to its contents. Having the index on cards makes it more convenient for use and for inserting cards for new books. The cards are filed in trays in one straight alphabetical arrangement. The printed ones are usually bought from the Library of Congress; the typewritten ones are prepared in your library. The label on the outside of each tray of the catalog cabinet indicates the part of the alphabet in that tray.

Guide Cards

At intervals through the catalog are *guide* cards, which stand up higher than the other cards. These indicate where to *begin looking* in the tray and are great time-savers.

Alphabetical Arrangement

Every book except literature (fiction, poetry, drama, essays, and so forth) *usually* has at least three cards in the catalog so that you may locate it by looking under the *author*, the *title*, or the *subject*. Obviously, these cards are filed separately wherever they belong in the alphabet. Alphabetical filing is by the first word not an article (*a, the, an,* or their equivalents in foreign languages), at the top of the card. Some filing practices are common to most libraries. For instance, author cards for books by the same author are

filed alphabetically by the words in the title, which appears immediately below the author's name. "See also" references appear *after* all cards on a subject, leading to additional information on related subjects. Abbreviations are filed as if spelled out—*Saint* for *St., Mister* for *Mr.,* and *Mac* for *Mc.* The German *umlaut* is filed as *oe* for *ö* and *ue* for *ü.*

Other variations in alphabetizing are the *word by word* method and the *letter by letter* method. This means that subject headings, authors' names, and titles of more than one word may be arranged in the alphabet either by considering each word separately or by considering all of the words together as one long word. For example:

Word by Word	*Letter by Letter*
Lay baptism	Lay baptism
Lay mass books	Laying on of hands
Lay ordination	Lay mass books
Lay patronage	Laymen
Lay preaching	Lay ordination
Lay readers	Lay patronage
Laying on of hands	Lay preaching
Laymen	Lay readers

Usually, card catalogs are alphabetized *word by word.*

The filing code or rules for the individual library must be consulted in a great many situations where variations are possible and acceptable. In filing the cards for a number of different *editions* of a book, some libraries place the latest edition *ahead* of all others. The subject cards for books on the history of a country are usually filed chronologically. The rule for hyphenated words often upsets the filing code of a library because of variations used by authors of books—for instance, *mass books* and *mass-books.*

Identical names are usually filed by dates:

> Knox, John, 1505–1572.
> Knox, John, 1900–

Numerals in the names of royalty or of religious hierarchy are filed numerically:

> Edward I, King of England, 1239–1307.
> Edward II, King of England, 1284–1327.
>
> Pius IX, pope, 1792–1878.
> Pius X, pope, 1835–1914.

Punctuation marks are disregarded, as are titles of honor.

Study carefully any "stamped" information on a card. It may indicate the location of a book or call attention to the *main entry* (usually the author card or its substitute). Always ask for information if your search leads you to a *temporary* card in the catalog—a colored card, usually "riding the rod." The use of a temporary card probably means that the regular cards have been removed from the catalog for revision. It does not necessarily indicate that the book is not available; so inform yourself as to the temporary-card system in your library.

Catalog Cards

Close attention to the catalog card will help you decide whether the book it represents is the one you want. It gives the author and title and indicates whether the book is written by one or more persons. It mentions the edition, if other than the first, and gives the *imprint* of the book—where it was published, the name of the publisher, and the date of publication. Noticing the number of pages in the book or the number of volumes is important; if the book is one of a set of books, be sure to add the number of the desired volume to the call number when requesting it or looking for it in an open-stack library. If the book is illustrated, the card will show the fact. Frequently, explanatory notes appear on the card—a very useful one being that noting a bibliography in the book. Then, near the bottom, you will find the *subjects* of the book listed, as an indication of other cards in the catalog for the same book. Also, you will find the order number and the printing number of the card, the Library of Congress Classification number, and the Dewey Decimal Classification number—most of which have no importance to the catalog user.

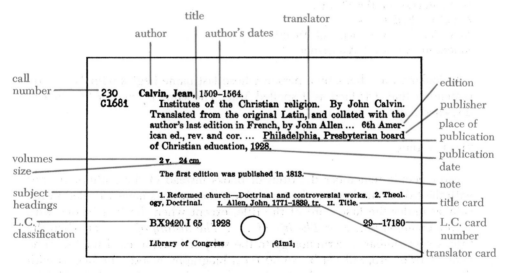

AUTHOR CARDS

The above card is an author card. To find a book by John Calvin, look under his *last name*, Calvin, for *Calvin, Jean* (you would already have followed a cross reference from *Calvin, John* to *Calvin, Jean*), which is the first line at the top of the card. The catalog lists those of his books which the library owns, each represented by a separate card.

If the library has more than one book by an author, the author cards are filed alphabetically by the words in the title, which appears just below the author's name. Books are listed under the author's real name, with a cross reference from his pseudonym (fictional name under which he writes) if he has one.

JOINT AUTHORS

If more than one person collaborate in writing a book, the main author card is under the author first mentioned on the title page of the book; another card is filed in the catalog for each *joint author*, whose name is typed above the main author's name.

CORPORATE ENTRIES

The government, an institution, an association, a society, a religious body, or a corporation may be considered the author of a publication issued in its name. Such name, instead of a person's name, appears in the author's place on the catalog card, and it is called a *corporate entry*. For instance:

U. S. Bureau of the Census
American Red Cross
New York (State) Dept. of Health
American Historical Association

In looking for a book by a person whose last name begins with *Mc* or *M',* remember that it is filed as if spelled *Mac.* The same is true for *St.,* filed as if spelled *Saint.*

TITLE CARDS

Most people remember the titles of books instead of the authors. A card with the title of the book at the top (above the author's name) is filed in the catalog under the first word of the title, except when the title begins with such a common phrase as *The life of* . . ., *The history of* . . ., or when the title is very similar in terminology to the subject heading used for the same book. A title card will not be found for a biography whose title begins with the name of the person about whom the book is written—*John Calvin, humanist and theologian.* Generally, the subject card suffices—listing the book under *Calvin, Jean, 1509–1564.*

An article (*a, the, an,* or the foreign equivalent) is never considered the first word of a title in filing. Thus, *The twentieth century Bible commentary* is filed under the word *twentieth.* Titles that contain numerals are filed as though the figures were written out: as *One hundred one prayers for peace* instead of *101 prayers for peace* or as *One hundred basic theological titles* instead of *100 basic theological titles.* Initials standing for names of organizations, and so forth, *when in titles,* are filed as initials and *not* as if spelled out.

The title card is *exactly* like the author card except that the title has been typed above the author's name, so that it may be filed in the correct alphabetical place for people looking for a book by its title.

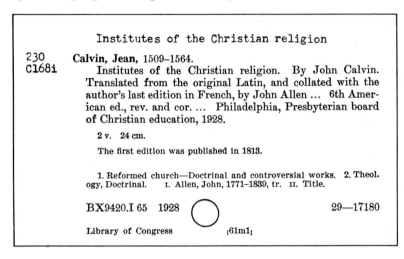

Institutes of the Christian religion

230
C168i   Calvin, Jean, 1509–1564.
         Institutes of the Christian religion. By John Calvin. Translated from the original Latin, and collated with the author's last edition in French, by John Allen ... 6th American ed., rev. and cor. ... Philadelphia, Presbyterian board of Christian education, 1928.

2 v.   24 cm.

The first edition was published in 1813.

1. Reformed church—Doctrinal and controversial works. 2. Theology, Doctrinal.   i. Allen, John, 1771–1839, tr.   ii. Title.

BX9420.I 65   1928   29—17180

Library of Congress   ₍61m1₎

SUBJECT CARDS

Often you will need material on a subject without knowing any authors or titles to consult. In that case, look under the *subject itself.* Be specific, not general, in looking up subject headings. For instance, look for *Pyramids,* not *Egypt—Antiquities;* or look for *Baptism,* not *Sacraments,* unless you really

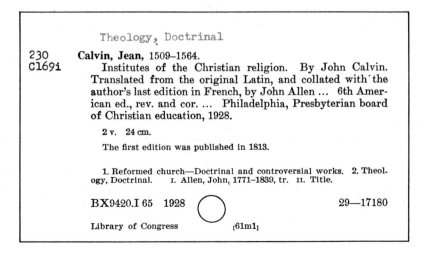

Theology, Doctrinal

230
C169i   Calvin, Jean, 1509–1564.
         Institutes of the Christian religion. By John Calvin. Translated from the original Latin, and collated with the author's last edition in French, by John Allen ... 6th American ed., rev. and cor. ... Philadelphia, Presbyterian board of Christian education, 1928.

2 v.   24 cm.

The first edition was published in 1813.

1. Reformed church—Doctrinal and controversial works. 2. Theology, Doctrinal.   i. Allen, John, 1771–1839, tr.   ii. Title.

BX9420.I 65   1928   29—17180

Library of Congress   ₍61m1₎

want material on the broader subject. These headings are typed in red on the top line of the card (above the author's name, just as on the title card). Otherwise, this card is *exactly* like the author card. Some libraries type the subject headings in black capital letters instead of red letters.

If the library has more than one book on a subject, all of the subject cards are together in the catalog, arranged alphabetically by the author's last name. For example: A subject card for a book on *Church history* by Archibald Gillies *Baker* will come before the one by Philip *Hughes*, which will come before the one by Louis Israel *Newman*.

SUBDIVIDED SUBJECT HEADINGS

Many subjects have *subdivisions*. They are arranged alphabetically in the catalog *after* the general subject heading:

Church history.
Church history—Addresses, essays, lectures.
Church history—Maps.
Church history—Modern period.
Church history—Philosophy.
Church history—Primitive and early church.
Church history—Primitive and early church—Addresses, essays, lectures.

INVERTED SUBJECTS

Some *phrase* subject headings (more than one word) are inverted to bring out the important word first; that is, *Hygiene, Hindu;* or *Hygiene, Jewish.* If the subject heading you are looking for cannot be found, look under a similar one. In most libraries, books on *World War I* are entered in the catalog under *European War, 1914–1918* (in red), with a cross reference from *World War I, 1914–1918;* but *World War II* is treated under *World War, 1939–1945.*

ANALYTICAL CARDS

Some libraries "analyze" the contents of a book of short stories, essays, or plays by different authors and prepare author and title cards for each one in the collection. *Subject analytics* are also prepared in some libraries for books whose chapters cover different subjects; a subject card is made for each *part* of the book dealing with a distinct subject. These *analytical cards* make each part of the book available to the users of the card catalog. However, with the increase in the number of published indexes to many such collections, the need for *analytics* has lessened.

PERIODICALS

Periodicals subscribed to by the library are represented in the card catalog under the title of the periodical. Some smaller libraries place immediately back of this card a *check-list* card showing the volumes owned by the library. However, the large libraries are discontinuing such a practice because of the immense cost of keeping this record up to date. Many periodicals have one title card in the catalog because all necessary information can be put on one card; but you will find many others which require two or more cards.

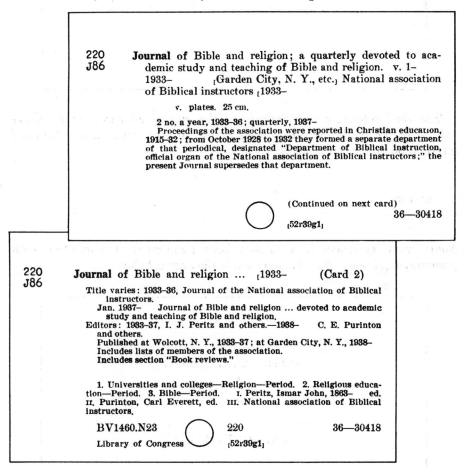

Sign Posts

Since it is impractical to file cards under every synonym of a given subject, cross references are provided to lead to the subject under which you will find the material for which you are looking.

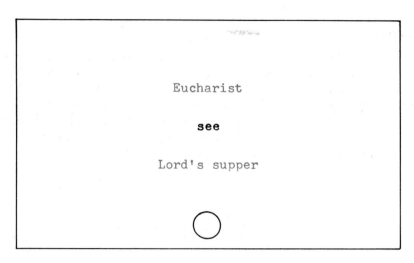

"See also" reference cards appear at the *end* of all cards on a *subject* (ahead of the cards for subdivisions of the subject) to lead to *additional* information on related subjects.

Episcopacy
    see also
Apostolic succession; Bishops; Dioceses; Methodism.

Name cross references have already been mentioned in connection with pseudonyms. (See p. 12.) Such a card is illustrated below.

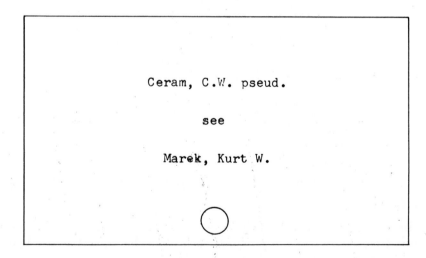

CALL NUMBERS

Every catalog card has the *call number* of the book in the upper left corner. It is wise, even in open-stack libraries, to fill out a call slip. If you cannot find the book on the shelf, it may have been charged out, may be misshelved, or may be lost. In such instances, the Circulation Desk needs the call slip to trace the book.

REFERENCE
BOOKS

Reference books have been mentioned several times in the preceding chapters; since the rest of this booklet is devoted to them, it may be wise to find out more about their characteristics. From our point of view, all books fall into two classes: those read for fun or for information, and those consulted for a definite fact, a piece of information, or a summary of some subject material. The latter are *reference books*. Of course, many more exist than can be treated here individually; but through the use of the library and with the Reference Librarian's help (or some other member of the professional staff), you will learn to know them and will find them useful.

Encyclopedias, both general and theological, should be used for an introductory, general survey of a subject. In a large library, however, reference books in special fields should be known and employed. Finding a set of encyclopedias on the reference shelf may be like meeting an old friend, but knowing how to use it is no reason for limiting your investigation to what it can offer.

Haphazard use of reference books wastes more time during the average educational experience than anything else. Unskillful searching frequently ends in failure unless a streak of sheer luck intervenes. Once the main points about these books are learned, selecting the proper book for a particular question will be easy. Attention to the following items should build up an automatic technique for the use of reference books.

Date

The date of a book is of first importance in locating information. For recent developments, like the emerging nations of the world, up-to-date books are necessary. In securing the latest edition of a book, remember that the "copyright" date on the back of the title page is your clue—not the date at the bottom of the title page.

Subjects Covered

If you are not familiar with the "scope" of a reference book, look through the introduction and the table of contents to see what it includes. Think of the college freshman who was earnestly "thumbing" through the current *Who's Who in America* for the life of George Washington. His technique was faulty in three respects: The book includes only living Americans (notice the title), and the fact that its items are alphabetically arranged makes "thumbing" unnecessary. The *date* was wrong, to begin with.

Arrangement

The articles in most reference books are alphabetically arranged for quick, easy location of material. If they are not so arranged, an alphabetical approach to the contents is provided—an index. However, many alphabetical books also have indexes, because the information is under large subjects, and the index is the key to small subjects treated as sub-topics under the large ones.

If the book itself does not have a key to abbreviations in it, their meanings can be found in a dictionary.

The Best Type of Reference Book

BIBLIOGRAPHIES

The best types of reference books include *bibliographies, signed articles,* and *cross references.* An article in a reference book is generally sufficient for the needs of the average person, but often it is not. A list of books (bibliography) at the end of an important article leads to further and more intensive reading on the subject. You don't have to be a research worker to realize the value of such bibliographies.

AUTHORITY

People who write articles for reference books are usually experts and specialists, and the best type of reference book gives the author's name at the end (occasionally, at the beginning) of each important article. Some give it in full; others give initials, for which identification may be made in the list of contributors in the front of the book. Obviously, this labeling lends authority to the book.

CROSS REFERENCES

Cross references have as much value in books as in card catalogs. An article cannot appear under every synonymous subject name. Therefore, it is entered under the one most people will think of, with cross references to it under the others. *See also* references help by leading to *additional* information. If you do not find cross references, don't assume that the book contains nothing on your subject. Look under as many synonymous subject titles as you can think of.

CARE

Reference books are very expensive public or institutional property and must be handled by many people; they should be used with care. Putting pencil marks in them, turning down the corners of pages, or rumpling the pages is highly inconsiderate of other users. Dropping the books may damage them a great deal.

Mutilation of books, reference books, magazines, and other library materials is a serious offense and a serious problem. Proper care of such materials is the responsibility of every individual—and theological students are not immune!

Selected References from
Index to Religious Periodical Literature
Vol. 4, 1957–1959

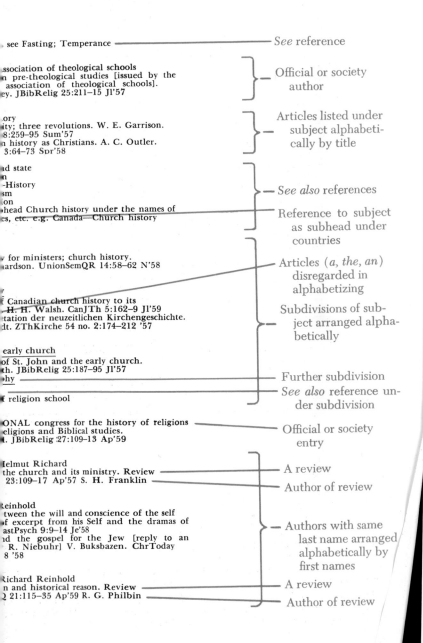

see Fasting; Temperance ————————— *See* reference

ssociation of theological schools
n pre-theological studies [issued by the
association of theological schools].
ey. JBibRelig 25:211–15 Jl'57
— Official or society
author

ory
ity; three revolutions. W. E. Garrison.
8:259–95 Sum'57
n history as Christians. A. C. Outler.
3:64–73 Spr'58
— Articles listed under
subject alphabeti-
cally by title

ad state
n
-History
sm
ion
head Church history under the names of
es, etc. e.g. Canada—Church history
— *See also* references

— Reference to subject
as subhead under
countries

for ministers; church history.
ardson. UnionSemQR 14:58–62 N'58
— Articles (*a, the, an*)
disregarded in
alphabetizing

f Canadian church history to its
H. H. Walsh. CanJTh 5:162–9 Jl'59
tation der neuzeitlichen Kirchengeschichte.
dt. ZThKirche 54 no. 2:174–212 '57
— Subdivisions of sub-
ject arranged alpha-
betically

early church
of St. John and the early church.
h. JBibRelig 25:187–95 Jl'57
hy
— Further subdivision
— *See also* reference under subdivision

f religion school

ONAL congress for the history of religions
eligions and Biblical studies.
J. JBibRelig 27:109–13 Ap'59
— Official or society
entry

Ielmut Richard
the church and its ministry. Review
23:109–17 Ap'57 S. H. Franklin
— A review
— Author of review

Leinhold
tween the will and conscience of the self
f excerpt from his Self and the dramas of
astPsych 9:9–14 Je'58
nd the gospel for the Jew [reply to an
R. Niebuhr] V. Buksbazen. ChrToday
8 '58
— Authors with same
last name arranged
alphabetically by
first names

Richard Reinhold
n and historical reason. Review
Q 21:115–35 Ap'59 R. G. Philbin
— A review
— Author of review

INDEXES

Periodical Indexes

Magazines contain much information that never appears in books or that is too recent to have been published in book form. So do newspapers. Some magazines are published every week, some every month, and others every two or three months. A certain number of these issues, usually covering six months, makes up a *volume;* the number of issues in a volume varies with different magazines. When a volume is complete, most libraries have it *bound* like a book, with an index to each volume.

Searching for information through the indexes in individual volumes of magazines would be a colossal task, taking more time than most people can spare. It would be like going to the shelves and searching among thousands of books to determine whether or not the library has the one you need. *An index to magazine material is just as necessary as an index to the book collection (the card catalog).* There are general indexes and specialized ones, and through them you may find articles on almost any subject or by almost any author.

All magazine indexes are alphabetically arranged: some by author, title, and subject like the card catalog; others, by author and subject; and still others, only by subject. Many of them are published monthly; but at intervals through the year, one issue will include not only the current month's index but will reprint *all in one alphabet* the indexes of the issues for two, three, or six months previous, so that you need to look in only one issue instead of in several. This is called a *cumulation*. Once a year each index cumulates for the whole year. For our further convenience, some indexes publish a two-year or a three-year cumulation. The *Index to Religious Periodical Literature* is now published annually, and *The Catholic Periodical Index* is published quarterly; both cumulate every two or three years.

Each entry in an index gives the name of the article; the author (if known); the name of the magazine in which it appeared; and the volume, pages, and exact date. For instance:

ECUMENICAL movement———————————— subject

Bibliography ————————————————— subdivision of subject

title of
article ——————— Bibliography for ministers; the ecumenical movement.

author ——————— R. T. Handy. UnionSemQR 14:44–9 My'59

                               name of   vol.   pages   date
                               magazine

For weekly periodicals, like *Christianity Today*, the day of the month is given with the month and the year:

Christianity Today 2:7–9 Ag 18 '58

You have no doubt noticed that the names of some of the magazines are abbreviated, as well as the names of months. This is done to save space. The full names of all magazines indexed appear in the front of each issue of the index and are usually checked as to the library's holdings. A key to abbreviations is also there. Many cross references, both *see* and *see also*, are used in indexes. (See pp. 15–16, 20.)

WHAT TO COPY

If you want the articles you have located through the index, copy very accurately the full name of the magazine, the volume number, the date, and (for your own benefit) the inclusive paging of the article.

Theological Periodical Indexes

Index to Religious Periodical Literature. Princeton, N. J., American Theological Library Assn., 1949–date. General index to periodical resources in the areas of religious and theological scholarship and related subjects. Basically Protestant, but includes selected Roman Catholic and Jewish journals. Ecumenical on both scholarly and popular levels; international in scope. Vol. 1—1949–1952; vol. 2—1953–1954; vol. 3—1955–1956 (not yet published, but still projected); vol. 4—1957–1959; annual vols. for 1960, 1961. The present policy is annual publication with cumulation every three years.

Arrangement: Author and subject index all in one alphabet. Articles *by* an author followed by articles *about* him. Subdivisions of subjects are underlined. Both annuals and cumulated volumes have book reviews indexed by author in second part of volume.

A

ABBA, Raymond
  Divine name Yahweh. JBibLit 80:320–8 D'61
ABERBACH, M.
  Change from a standing to a sitting posture by students after the death of Rabban Gamaliel. JewQR ns52: 168–74 O'61
ABILITIES, Special see Aptitudes
ABORIGINES see Native races
ABORTION
  Abortion in Norway; a comment. F. Littell. ChrCris 21: 27–8 Mr 6 '61
  Schwangerschaftsunterbrechung als religiöses und erzieherisches Problem [with biblio] H.J.Gamm. ZEvEthik 5:193–203 Jl'61
ABRAHAM, the patriarch
  Religion of Israel before Sinai. M.H.Segal. JewQR ns52:41–68 Jl'61
ABRAHAM in art
  Iconography of the Sacrifice of Abraham [with illus and catalog of the monuments] I.S. van Woerden. VigChr 15:214–55 F'61
ABRAMOWSKI, Luise
  Zur Theologie Theodors von Mopsuestia. ZKirchG 72 no 3–4:263–93 '61
ABRECHT, Paul Robert
  Communism in areas of rapid social change. ChrCris 21:171–4+ O 16'61
ABŪ 'ABD ALLĀH MUḤAMMAD ibn 'Alī al-Ḥakīm al-Tirmidhī see Muḥammad ibn 'Alī, Abū 'Abd Allāh, al-Tirmidhī
ACTON, John Emerich Edward Dalberg Acton, 1st baron
  Liberty, church and state; Gladstone's relations with Manning and Acton, 1832–1870. M.D.Stephen. JReligHist 1:217–32 D'61
ACTS of Thomas see Bible. New Testament (Books and parts)
  Apocryphal books. Acts of Thomas
ADAM, Alfred
  Die ursprüngliche Sprache der Salomo-Oden. ZNeutW 52 no 3–4:141–56 '61
ADAMS, James Luther
  Ernst Troeltsch as analyst of religion. JSSRelig 1:98– 109 O'61
ADOLESCENCE
  Understanding the adolescent offender. D.M.Simms. JPastCare 15:95–100 Sum'61
AETHERIA see Peregrinatio Aetheriae
AFFLICTION
    see also
  Good and evil
  Suffering
AFRICA
  Day of Africa. E.R.Martin. RvEx 58:105–17 Ja'61
    see also
  Africa--Law
  Missions--Africa
  Bibliography
  Continuing discussion. ChrCris 21:43 Mr 20 '61
  Nationalism
  Africa of the sixties. B. Ige. ChrCris 21:35–7 Mr 20 '61
  Danger of disillusionment with Africa. R.C.Good. ChrCris 21:30–4 Mr 20 '61
  Our faltering UN strategy on Africa. G.M.Houser. ChrCris 21:38–41 Mr 20 '61

Politics and go
  Danger of
    ChrCr
  Race problems
  Africa grov
    SocAct
      see
    Negro
AFRICA, East
  Politics and go
    Political d
      ChrCr
AFRICA, North
  Church history
    History and
      JThStu
    "Seniores i
      Africa
AFRICA, South
AFRICA, West
  West Africa
    71–3 M
      see
  Islam--
AGADA see Agga
AGED
  Health care
    Mr'61
  Medical ca
    121–2 ,
AGGADA
  Haggada wi
    22 Je'6
  Meaning of
    Jud 10:
AGNON, Samuel
  Jewish exis
    whole I
    16 Sum
AGRICOLA, Rud
  Melanchtho
  Heidell
  Archiv
AGRICULTURE,
  Israel
  Kvutza in c
AGUS, Irving A.
  Preconcept
    JewQR
AHARONI, Yohan
  Excavation
    D'61
AHERN, Barnaba
  Christian's
    and Ro
AHIKAR
  Les prover
    178–94
AHMADIYYAH m
  Apologetic
    tions fo
    Muslin
'AI, Palestine
  "Ai which i
    identity

ABSTINE

AMERICA
  Statemer
    Amer
  J. A.

CHURCH
  Church's
    Encou
  Our com
    Breth
      see
    Churc
    Inquis
    Missio
    Monas
    Refor
    also
    cou

Bibliograph
  Bibliogra
    C. C.

Historiogra
  Challeng
    histori
  Die Inte
    M. Sch

Primitive a
  Apocalyp
    P. K.
  Historiog
    see
    Histor

INTERNA
  History
  N. E.

NIEBUHR
  Purpose
  JapChi

NIEBUHR
  Dialogue
  [reprin
  history
  Niebuhr
  article
  3:10–2

NIEBUHR
  Resurrec
  CathB

Explanation

Sample title: Danger of disillusionment with Africa
Mr 20 '61.

Explanation: An article with the title given, written
Christianity and Crisis, volume 21, pages 30–34, in t

(The Index page is reprinted by permission from
Religious Periodical Literature, published by the A
ciation, with Editorial Office located at Princeton
New Jersey.)

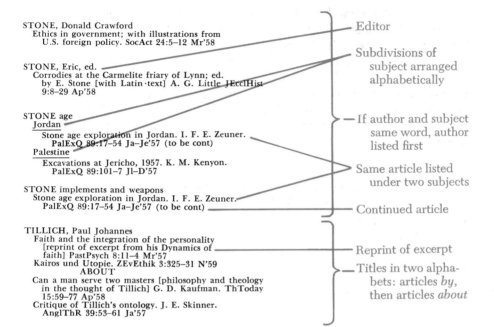

STONE, Donald Crawford
    Ethics in government; with illustrations from
        U.S. foreign policy. SocAct 24:5–12 Mr'58

STONE, Eric, ed.
    Corrodies at the Carmelite friary of Lynn; ed.
        by E. Stone [with Latin text] A. G. Little JEcclHist
        9:8–29 Ap'58

STONE age
    Jordan
        Stone age exploration in Jordan. I. F. E. Zeuner.
            PalExQ 89:17–54 Ja–Je'57 (to be cont)
    Palestine
        Excavations at Jericho, 1957. K. M. Kenyon.
            PalExQ 89:101–7 Jl–D'57

STONE implements and weapons
    Stone age exploration in Jordan. I. F. E. Zeuner.
        PalExQ 89:17–54 Ja–Je'57 (to be cont)

TILLICH, Paul Johannes
    Faith and the integration of the personality
        [reprint of excerpt from his Dynamics of
        faith] PastPsych 8:11–4 Mr'57
    Kairos und Utopie. ZEvEthik 3:325–31 N'59
            ABOUT
    Can a man serve two masters [philosophy and theology
        in the thought of Tillich] G. D. Kaufman. ThToday
        15:59–77 Ap'58
    Critique of Tillich's ontology. J. E. Skinner.
        AnglThR 39:53–61 Ja'57

Editor

Subdivisions of
    subject arranged
    alphabetically

If author and subject
    same word, author
    listed first

Same article listed
    under two subjects

Continued article

Reprint of excerpt

Titles in two alpha-
    bets: articles *by*,
    then articles *about*

The Catholic Periodical Index. Haverford, Pa., Catholic Library Association, 1930–date. A cumulative author and subject index to a selected list of Catholic periodicals, international in scope. Published quarterly— April and October cover three-month periods; July and December cover six months, replacing the two quarterly issues. The bound volume cumulates for two years, all in one alphabet, and uses *sa* for many *see also* references as a space-saving device. Individual poems are listed under POEMS, alphabetically arranged by author; and book reviews are listed under the author's name.

Selected References from *The Catholic Periodical Index*
January 1959–December 1960, July 1961

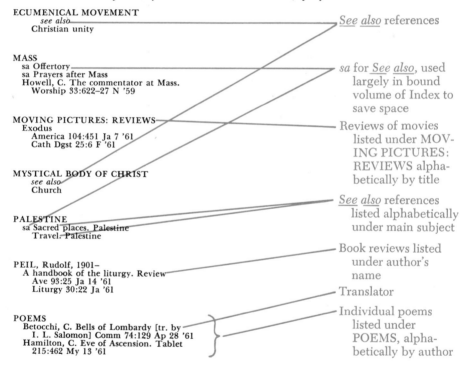

ECUMENICAL MOVEMENT
    see also
    Christian unity

See also references

MASS
    sa Offertory
    sa Prayers after Mass
    Howell, C. The commentator at Mass.
        Worship 33:622–27 N '59

sa for *See also*, used largely in bound volume of Index to save space

MOVING PICTURES: REVIEWS
    Exodus
        America 104:451 Ja 7 '61
        Cath Dgst 25:6 F '61

Reviews of movies listed under MOVING PICTURES: REVIEWS alphabetically by title

MYSTICAL BODY OF CHRIST
    see also
    Church

See also references listed alphabetically under main subject

PALESTINE
    sa Sacred places. Palestine
    Travel. Palestine

Book reviews listed under author's name

PEIL, Rudolf, 1901–
    A handbook of the liturgy. Review
    Ave 93:25 Ja 14 '61
    Liturgy 30:22 Ja '61

Translator

POEMS
    Betocchi, C. Bells of Lombardy [tr. by
        I. L. Salomon] Comm 74:129 Ap 28 '61
    Hamilton, C. Eve of Ascension. Tablet
        215:462 My 13 '61

Individual poems listed under POEMS, alphabetically by author

Guide to Catholic Literature. ed. by J. W. Sprug and J. A. Placek. Haverford, Pa., Catholic Library Association, 1960—date. (vols. 1–5, 1888–1959, ed. by Walter Romig. Grosse Point, Mich., Walter Romig, 1955–1959). An annotated author, title, and subject index in one alphabet to books and pamphlets by Catholics or of particular Catholic interest, American and of foreign countries. The latter ordinarily entered by author and subject. The subject headings correspond to those used in *The Catholic Periodical Index*. A significant development in the guide is author and subject analytics (see p. 14). A checklist of books so treated is in the back.

Vol. 1 is for 1888–1940, then every four years; from 1960, published annually. (This is not a magazine index, but it seems appropriate here with the above index.)

Christian Periodical Index, A Selected List: A Subject Index to Periodical Literature, 1956–1960, prepared by Librarians of the Christian Librarians' Fellowship. Buffalo, Buffalo Bible Institute Bookstore, 1961. Indexes 18 periodicals of interest to evangelical Bible institutes, seminaries, and Christian colleges. Does not include any titles appearing in Wilson indexes or, for the most part, in the *Index to Religious Periodical Literature*. Purely a subject index, does not include book reviews. A key to abbreviations is in the front, with an explanation of a sample entry.

An Alphabetical Subject Index and Index Encyclopaedia to Periodical Articles on Religion, 1890–1899, comp. and ed. by E. C. Richardson. New York, Scribner, c1907, 1911. Two volumes. World coverage; vol. 1, published in 1907, is a subject index, giving brief definition, good encyclopedia references on each subject to orient the reader in background. Bibliographic form brief. Vol. 2, 1911, is an author index. Full references given, but user must refer to the front of vol. 1 (subject index) for the list of periodicals indexed.

Religious and Theological Abstracts. (See p. 37.)

Biblical Subject Index. (See p. 73.)

The Methodist Periodical Index. Nashville, Tenn., Methodist Publishing House, 1962–date. An author and subject index to articles published in Methodist periodicals, including book reviews, stories, poems, and news items. This index replaces *The Periodical Key*, ed. and published by B. J. Clark, which was published through April 1960 and completed with the issue of vol. 2, no. 5.

Index Islamicus, 1906–1955, comp. by J. D. Pearson and J. F. Ashton. Cambridge, England, W. Heffner, c1958. A catalog of articles on Islamic subjects in periodicals and other collective publications. In front: list of sources and list of abbreviations; in back, author index.

General Periodical Indexes

Readers' Guide to Periodical Literature. 1900–date. New York, Wilson, 1905–date. This is the most used general periodical index. Its field is general, covering all subjects, and it indexes magazines from 1900 to the present time. Originally it included about 15 of the most popular magazines; now, more than 100. It is published twice a month except during July and August, when there is just one for each month. The second issue each month includes what has been published in the first one, all in one alphabet. This cumulation keeps the index up to date and makes it unnecessary to look in two issues. This is true of the three-month cumulations also. The bound yearly volume takes the place of the paper ones for twelve months.

The arrangement is alphabetical, articles being entered under author and subject, and under title when necessary. Title entries are made for stories and plays, and occasionally for essays. Titles of poems are given under the subject "Poems."

Poole's Index to Periodical Literature, 1802–1907. Boston, Houghton Mifflin, 1893–1908. An index to subjects only—no author entries. The ancestor of all magazine indexes, it is the only index to nineteenth-century periodicals up to 1890. *Poole's* does not give the date in the entry for an article—only the volume and the paging. The date can be computed from a table in the front of the index if it is needed.

Nineteenth Century Readers' Guide to Periodical Literature, 1890–1899, with supplementary indexing, 1900–1922. New York, Wilson, 1944. 2 volumes. In contrast to *Poole's Index,* this includes author and illustrator entries as well as subject entries, and title entries to short stories, novels, plays, and poems. Book reviews are well indexed.

International Index, A Quarterly Guide to Periodical Literature in the Social Sciences and Humanities. New York, Wilson, 1907–date. The title and content of this index have changed from time to time: 1907–March 1955: *International Index to Periodicals;* April 1955–March 1957: *International Index, A Guide to Periodical Literature in Social Sciences and Humanities.* Beginning in June 1955, scientific, psychological, and foreign-language periodicals were dropped.

It is now an author and subject index to more scholarly journals in the social sciences and the humanities, including religion and philosophy. Issued quarterly and cumulated every two years since 1958; prior to that date, it cumulated every three years.

Bibliographic Index; A Cumulative Bibliography of Bibliographies. 1937/42–date. New York, Wilson, 1938–date. An alphabetical subject index to separately published bibliographies as well as to bibliographies appearing in books and periodicals, including many foreign titles. Published quarterly, with annual cumulation in March and further cumulation every four years.

A key to periodical abbreviations and one for general abbreviations in front.

Selected References from the *International Index, A Quarterly Guide to Periodical Literature in the Social Sciences and Humanities* April 1958–March 1960, March 1961, June 1961

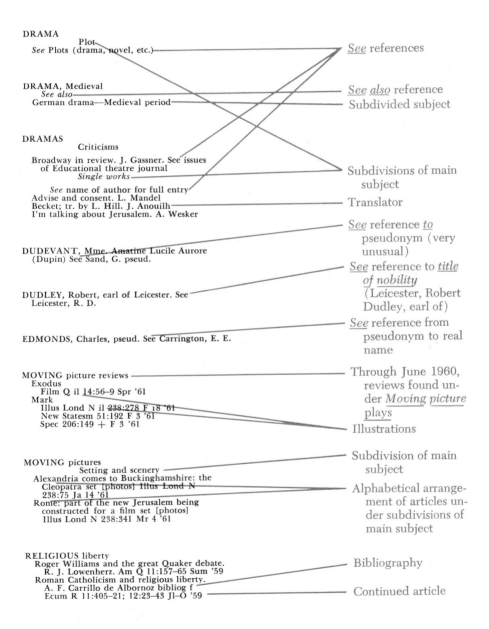

DRAMA
    Plot
    See Plots (drama, novel, etc.)

See references

DRAMA, Medieval
    See also
    German drama—Medieval period

See also reference
Subdivided subject

DRAMAS
    Criticisms
    Broadway in review. J. Gassner. See issues
       of Educational theatre journal
          Single works
    See name of author for full entry
    Advise and consent. L. Mandel
    Becket; tr. by L. Hill. J. Anouilh
    I'm talking about Jerusalem. A. Wesker

Subdivisions of main
   subject
Translator

See reference *to*
   pseudonym (very
   unusual)

DUDEVANT, Mme. Amatine Lucile Aurore
    (Dupin) See Sand, G. pseud.

See reference to *title of nobility*
   (Leicester, Robert
   Dudley, earl of)

DUDLEY, Robert, earl of Leicester. See
    Leicester, R. D.

See reference from
   pseudonym to real
   name

EDMONDS, Charles, pseud. See Carrington, E. E.

MOVING picture reviews
    Exodus
       Film Q il 14:56–9 Spr '61
    Mark
       Illus Lond N il 238:278 F 18 '61
       New Statesm 51:192 F 3 '61
       Spec 206:149 + F 3 '61

Through June 1960,
   reviews found un-
   der *Moving picture plays*

Illustrations

MOVING pictures
    Setting and scenery
    Alexandria comes to Buckinghamshire: the
       Cleopatra set [photos] Illus Lond N
       238:75 Ja 14 '61
    Rome: part of the new Jerusalem being
       constructed for a film set [photos]
       Illus Lond N 238:341 Mr 4 '61

Subdivision of main
   subject

Alphabetical arrange-
   ment of articles un-
   der subdivisions of
   main subject

RELIGIOUS liberty
    Roger Williams and the great Quaker debate.
       R. J. Lowenherz. Am Q 11:157–65 Sum '59
    Roman Catholicism and religious liberty.
       A. F. Carrillo de Albornoz bibliog f
       Ecum R 11:405–21; 12:23–43 Jl–O '59

Bibliography

Continued article

RELIGIOUS literature
  Religious book section. il Times Lit Sup
    2934:sup i–xii My 23 '58; 2977:sup i–xvi
    Mr 20 '59 ————————————————— Illustrations

                               Works listed under
SAND, George, pseud. of Mme. Dudevant   pseudonym instead
  Heine's letter to Bacage, September 11,   of real name
  1855. S. Atkins. Mod Lang Q 20:74–6   (unusual)
  Mr '59

SHORT stories ————————————————— *See* reference
  See name of author for full entry
    English language ———————————— Subdivision of main
  Balance of nature. K. Reeves   subject
  I need a friend. E. Berridge
  Transgression. S. Karchmer ————————— Only titles and
                                   authors listed here

Newspaper Index

New York Times Index. New York, New York Times, 1913–date. A subject index to the New York *Times*. From 1913 to 1929 it was published four times a year, then monthly, and now it is published twice each month, with a yearly volume. An added feature is a list of News Highlights of the year which precedes the actual index.

Each entry gives exact reference to the day (not the year, because the index never cumulates for more than one year), page, and column; for Sunday, it gives the section also. The following references were located through a cross reference *from* "Dead Sea Scrolls" *to* "Bible": °

> BIBLE
>   Dead Sea Scrolls; Prof Walther draws on material
> from Scrolls in questioning Holy Wk chronology, Soc of
> Biblical Literature and Exegesis, Ja 1, 26:1
>   Dead Sea Scrolls; Prof Zeitlin Ir on Mar 28 rept holds
> use of certain symbols indicates Scrolls could not have
> been written in pre-Christian period, Ap 6, IV, 8:6

The first article appeared in the New York *Times* of January 1 (1959), page 26, column 1. The second article was for April 6 (1959), section 4, page 8, column 6.

The *New York Times Index* does not give the *title* of the article (headline) but a summary or abstract, concise and informative. It is a day-by-day history of the world. Alphabetical word by word, under subjects and personal and organization names. Utilizes many cross references. The index can be used for other newspapers for national and international news by using the *date*.

Other Indexes

EDUCATION

Education Index. New York, Wilson, 1929–date. An author and subject index to educational literature, including magazines, books, pamphlets, re-

° Copyright by The New York Times. Reprinted by permission.

ports, and so forth. It is published monthly except in July and August. Cumulates four times yearly, with annual and biennial volumes in June. Another useful index is *Research Studies in Education,* Bloomington, Indiana, Phi Kappa Delta, 1941–1951,—a subject-field index of doctoral dissertations, reports, and field studies, with a Research Methods bibliography. Annual.

PSYCHOLOGY

Psychological Index, 1894–1935, ed. by H. C. Warren, C. L. Vaughan, W. S. Hunter, and others. Princeton, N. J., Psychological Review Co., c1895–1936. 42 volumes. Subtitle is "An Annual Bibliography of the Literature of Psychology and Cognate Subjects." Lists original publications in all languages. Classified by subject, with an author index. A list of periodicals indexed, with their abbreviations, is given in vol. 30. Publication discontinued, but work carried on by *Psychological Abstracts.*

Psychological Abstracts. Lancaster, Pa., American Psychological Association, 1927–date. Lists new books and articles, grouped by subject. Very important is the signed abstract or summary of each item. Universal in scope, abstracts in English. Author index to each issue and detailed subject index to each volume. Now replaces *Psychological Index.* Published every two months, cumulates annually.

Psychological Abstracts: Abstract References. ed. by H. L. Ansbacher. Columbus, Ohio, American Psychological Association, 1940, 1941. 2 volumes. Covers the period 1894–1928. Its use precedes and is a backward extension of *Psychological Abstracts.*

PUBLIC AFFAIRS

Public Affairs Information Service. New York, Public Affairs Information Service, 1915–date. A *subject* index to the fields of sociology, economics, and political science—from the practical side particularly. Indexes not only periodicals, but books, documents, pamphlets, and reports of public and private agencies relating to economic and social conditions, public administration, and international relations published in English throughout the world. Commonly called *P.A.I.S.*

Published weekly from September through July, fortnightly during August. Cumulates five times yearly, the fifth being the annual volume.

ART

Art Index. New York, Wilson, 1929–date. An author and subject index to fine arts periodicals and museum bulletins. Issued quarterly, with an annual volume in October.

BIOGRAPHY

Biography Index. 1946–date. New York, Wilson, 1948–date. A one-place index to biographical material in books and magazines, universal in scope. It has two sections: an alphabetical name index, and an index to professions and occupations, alphabetical by subject. Published quarterly, with an annual volume in August.

BOOKS

Book Review Digest. New York, Wilson, 1905–date. Digested reviews of current books with references to full reviews. Issued monthly except during February and July, it cumulates at each half-year (August) and in an annual volume in February. Alphabetical by author, with a title and subject index. The following is an example of a reference from the *Book Review Digest:*

> MacLeish, Archibald. J.B.; a play in verse. 153 p. $3.50
> Houghton
>
> A poetic drama based on the Book of Job retelling the old story of man's questioning of God's goodness in modern dress.
>
> Library J 82:3113 D 1 '57 60 w
> N Y Times p3 Mr 23 '58 650 w
> Sat R 41:11 Mr 8 '58 2000 w

Archibald MacLeish is the author. *J.B.; A Play in Verse* is the title of the book, 153 pages, priced at $3.50, published by Houghton. A brief annotation or summary of the book follows, then the condensed reviews which lead to the full reviews by giving the name of the magazine, volume, page, date, and length of the review—for instance, 60 words.

Cumulative Book Index, ed. by Mary Burnham and Regina Goldman; managing editor, Carol Hurd. New York, Wilson, 1929–date. A world list of books in the English language. Issued monthly except in August, it cumulates in July and in December. Periodically it cumulates for a number of years; all such volumes since 1928 are supplements to the *United States Catalog.* Alphabetically arranged by author, title, and subject.

DRAMA

Dramatic Index, 1909–1949. Boston, Faxon, 1910–1952. An index to theatrical *articles* in American and English *periodicals,* covering the stage and screen. Alphabetical by subject and title. No longer published, it appeared quarterly in the *Bulletin of Bibliography* and annually with the *Magazine Subject Index.*

Index to Plays, 1800–1926; Supplement, 1927–1934, by I. T. E. Firkins. New York, Wilson, 1927, 1935. An index to many thousands of plays appearing in collections and elsewhere, arranged in two parts: an author index with full information, and then a title and subject index. In the back are two lists of *collections* of plays indexed.

Index to Full Length Plays, by R. G. Thompson. Boston, Faxon, 1946, 1957. In two volumes, one covering 1895–1925, another covering 1926–1944. Each contains three indexes—to authors, to titles, and to subjects—with full information about each play in the title index, to which the author and subject indexes refer. The subject index is most useful.

Index to One-Act Plays, by Hannah Logasa and Winifred Ver Nooy. Boston, Faxon, 1924–1958. Five volumes—basic volume with four supplements—cover the period from 1900 through 1957 (the last two include radio plays). The fourth supplement, 1948–1957, is by Hannah Logasa only. Alphabetical by title, with an author and a subject index.

Play Index, 1949–1952, by D. H. West and D. M. Peake. New York, Wilson, 1953. A newer index which augments but does not supersede Firkins' *Index to Plays* and its supplements. (Logasa and Ottemiller will still be necessary for the periods and special types covered.)

Arranged in four parts: (1) main list, arranged by author, title, and subject (full information under author); (2) list of the collections indexed; (3) cast analysis, a new feature listing each play under the type of cast (male, female, mixed, and puppet) and by number of characters; (4) directory of publishers. Indexes all kinds of plays, including radio and TV plays, for both adults and children.

Index to Plays in Collections, 1900–1926, by J. H. Ottemiller. Washington, D. C., Scarecrow Press, 1951. Author and title index to plays from ancient to modern times.

LITERATURE

Four of the best indexes in the field of historical literature are: *American Historical Association's Guide to Historical Literature* (See p. 42); *Guide to the Best Fiction*, by E. A. Baker and James Packman, New York, Macmillan, 1932; *Guide to Historical Fiction*, by E. A. Baker and James Packman, New York, Macmillan, 1914; *Guide to the Best Historical Novels and Tales*, by Jonathan Nield, New York, Macmillan, 1929.

Essay and General Literature Index, 1900–date. Ed. by M. E. Sears and Marian Shaw. New York, Wilson, 1934–date. An author, subject, and title (when necessary) index to essays and articles published since 1900. It first appeared in 1934, covering 1900–1933. Since then, publication has occurred twice a year, the second being the annual volume. In the back of the index is a list of books indexed, checked for the library's holdings.

Short Story Index, by D. E. Cook and I. S. Munro. New York, Wilson, 1953. *Supplement, 1950–1954*. 1956. Supersedes Firkins' *Index to Short Stories*, 1923, and its supplements, 1929, 1936. Indexed by author, title, and, in many cases, subject, all in one alphabet, with full information under author. Pt. 2 is a list of collections indexed, by author and title.

Granger's Index to Poetry, ed. by W. F. Bernhardt. 5th ed., rev. and enl. New York, Columbia University Press, 1962. Arrangement in three parts: (1) title and first line index, (2) author index, (3) subject index, greatly expanded in this edition. Editions earlier than 1953 are useful for the indexing of anthologies omitted in later editions. The title formerly was *Index to Poetry and Recitations.*

Other Useful Indexes

Fiction Index, ed. by G. B. Cotton. London, Association of Assistant Librarians, 1953. Almost entirely English, published in England.

Music Index. Detroit, Mich., Information Service, 1949–date. Monthly, with annual cumulation.

Song Index, by M. E. Sears. New York, Wilson, 1926, 1934. 1926, with a 1934 supplement. Contains titles, first lines, and composers' and authors' names in one alphabet.

Speech Index, 1900–1933; Supplement, 1933–1955, by R. B. Sutton. New York, Wilson, 1935; New Brunswick, N. J., Scarecrow Press, 1956. Guide to the better-known speeches of famous orators and to types of speeches. Arrangement by author, subject, and type of speech.

Subject Index to Periodicals, 1915–1922; 1926–date. London, Library Association, 1919–date. English publication, useful for some English local-history periodicals and for the publications of important antiquarian societies. As of 1962, new title is *British Humanities Index.*

Ulrich's Periodicals Directory, ed. by E. C. Graves. 10th ed. New York, Bowker, 1962. Classified guide to a selected list of current periodicals, domestic and foreign.

THEOLOGICAL
ABSTRACTING
TOOLS

Abstracting magazines or journals are publications which not only index the contents of other magazines, but also give additional information in the form of a summary or abstract of the articles they cover. They can be thought of as being in the same category of reference tools as periodical indexes, although they are obviously more informative. The title of an article located through a periodical index might show promise of information which is not in the article. However, you could soon see by reading an *abstract* whether you need to find the original article to read in its entirety, or whether the title was misleading or the article insufficient for your purpose.

The entries in abstracting periodicals are similar to those in periodical indexes in that they are usually entered by author, followed by the title of the article and the title of the periodical in which it appears, volume, and paging. The abstract of the article follows.

Scientists in particular have long used abstracting journals, such as *Chemical Abstracts,* in order to cover the voluminous material published in chemistry, physics, biology, and related fields. There are abstracting journals in other fields as well, such as *Psychological Abstracts,* but those in the area of theology and religion are relatively recent in their beginning.

Religious and Theological Abstracts. Youngstown, Ohio, Theological Publications, Inc., 1958–date. Vol. 1–2, 1957–1958; vol. 3–4, 1959–1960. Published quarterly in March, June, September, and December by a non-sectarian abstracting service in cooperation with the editors of journals abstracted. A typical abstracting tool, foreign works included, but all abstracts are in English. Each issue is divided into four classified sections—Biblical, Theological, Historical, and Practical—which are in turn subdivided. Entries are numbered and there is a subject, author, and scripture index in the final

37

issue of each volume (cumulates every two years). There is a list of journals abstracted and abbreviations used in the back of each issue.

Abstractors are not given; but where possible, the location and position of the author of the original article is given in brackets after his name. This latter feature is often quite useful if the author is not well known. Some of the journals abstracted are not given complete coverage; only those articles which are relevant to religion and theology are abstracted.

New Testament Abstracts. Weston, Mass., Weston College of the Holy Spirit, 1956–. This tool appears three times a year. As in the above title, each issue is arranged by subject, has numbered entries, and includes abstracts of book reviews also. The index appears in the last issue of each volume and is extremely thorough. A list of journals abstracted and a list of abstractors is provided.

Studia Liturgica; An International Ecumenical Quarterly for Liturgical Research and Renewal. Rotterdam, Studia Liturgica, 1962–. This is a new periodical which has articles published in English. Although not primarily an abstracting journal, it contains in each issue a bibliography of new materials on liturgiology in the form of index cards. Each item in the bibliography is an abstract of an article or of a book.

Internationale Zeitschriftenschau für Bibelwissenschaft und Grenzgebiete. Stuttgart, Verlag Katholisches Bibelwerk, 1951/52–. This tool is for the more linguistically gifted students who will find it useful. English and non-English abstracts of many periodical articles. The title page is in French and in English as well as in German. The English title is *International Review of Biblical Studies.*

Theologische Literaturzeitung. Berlin, Verlag der Evangelischen Verlagsanstalt, 1876–. This one is generally limited to book reviews, in German.

BIBLIOGRAPHIES

The theological student cannot get very far in his study without the aid of bibliographies (See page 100) in one form or another, for they are indispensable for the beginner and the scholar alike. The term "bibliography" is used here to mean a list of books, pamphlets, writings, and so forth, relating to a given subject or by an author. Such lists are found in various forms and in various places. They can be extremely brief, listing only *author* and *short title,* or they can be fuller, giving also *place, publisher,* and *date.* Often the lists have annotations describing the contents and arrangement of the books included, as well as notes evaluating the use of the book and comparing its value with that of others on the same subject.

The card catalog itself is in a sense a bibliography, although a general one, for it locates for the user of a particular library the books directly on the subject which are contained in that library. Furthermore, bibliographies on special subjects to be found in the library can be located through the card catalog.

Many scholarly treatises (histories, Biblical studies, commentaries, encyclopedia and dictionary articles, and so forth) include some sort of bibliography at the end of individual chapters, divisions, or entries or at the end of the work to provide background and further source materials for supplementary reading.

Our main concern here, however, is with specialized subject bibliographies published separately. A few selected ones are listed merely to represent the variety available to the theological student.

General Theology

A Bibliography of Bibliographies in Religion, by J. G. Barrow. Ann Arbor, Mich., Edwards Brothers, 1955. Brings together all separately published bibliographies in the field of religion. Symbols indicate where copies were seen and where other copies have been reported. Exhaustive index in the back. Under each subject or subdivision bibliographies are listed in chronological order by dates of published works on the same subject of the same year, arranged in alphabetical order. Undated works in alphabetical order at ends of sections.

International Bibliography of the History of Religions for the Year, 1952–, by Henrietta Boas. Leyden, E. J. Brill, 1954. Annual volumes through 1956, 1957 have been published, with regular volumes for later years anticipated. Books are divided into three parts: General Works, Phenomenology of Religions, and History of Religions. Attempts to give as complete a list as possible of the books and articles relating to the history of religions which were published during the year under review, as well as book reviews appearing during the period. Omits such fields as the Old Testament, the New Testament, and Folklore, since these areas are well covered in specialized bibliographies. List of abbreviations in front; no index.

Bibliographia Ad Usum Seminarioum, ed. by Dr. Mag. Luchesius Smits. Nijmegen, Holland, Bestelcentrale der V. S. K. B., 1960–. A new series, of which two volumes have appeared and thirteen more are projected, each volume to be devoted to one of the principal and minor subjects usually taught in theological and philosophical seminaries (Roman Catholic). Each volume issued in three editions—English, German, and French. A selected, well-annotated bibliography, arranged in six or eight chapters with subheads in each. Includes only those works considered as indispensable or at least of considerable value for general or specialized knowledge of the subject. "Index of contents" (really table of contents) and an index of authors at the end of each volume.

Already published: Vol. 1—*Critical Bibliography of Liturgical Literature,* by Th. A. Vismans and Lucas Brinkhoff, tr. by R. W. Fitzpatrick and Clifford Howell. Vol. 2—*Critical Bibliography of Missiology,* by Livinus Vriens, with collaboration of Anastasius Disch and J. Wils, tr. by Deodatus Tummers. Announced volumes in English are: Vol. 3—*Critical Bibliography of Canon Law;* Vol. 4—*Critical Bibliography of Empirical Psychology;* Vol. 5—*Critical Bibliography of Sociology;* Vol. 6—*Critical Bibliography of Biblical Literature.*

Livres Catholiques. Paris, Lethielleux, 1945–1958. Thus far, in three volumes—1945–1951, 1951–1955, 1955–1958. Lists new books and reprints, arranged in fifteen divisions with subdivisions, giving format, paging, editor, price, and so forth. The indexes are by author, by title, and by publisher's series.

Guide to Catholic Literature. (See p. 28.)

The Catholic Bookman's Guide; A Critical Evaluation of Catholic Literature, ed. by Sister M. Regis, foreword by F. X. Canfield. New York, Hawthorn Books, c1962. Provides authoritative, comprehensive and up-to-date aid in selecting literature in many subject fields which meets the needs and interests of the Catholic point of view.

An evaluating essay, signed by its author at the beginning, introduces each category of literature, followed by extensive bibliographical references currently in print in English, each evaluated. In the front is a section on professional biography of contributors. In the back is a directory of publishers, American and foreign, followed by a full index. Arranged by subject fields.

Catholic Periodicals of Theological Interest, by F. L. Sheerin. Princeton, N. J., American Theological Library Association Newsletter, Nov. 15, 1958. 1958. A classified, selective list of 247 Catholic periodicals. Many foreign-language ones included. Some annotations; index of titles at the end.

A Baptist Bibliography by E. C. Starr. Chester, Pa., American Baptist Historical Society, 1947-1962—. In progress, 8 volumes having been published. A register of printed material by and about Baptists, including works written against the Baptists. Designed primarily for Baptists but useful to other denominations. Alphabetical by author with a title index.

Essential Books for a Pastor's Study; Basic and Recommended Works, by the Faculty of Union Theological Seminary. 3rd ed. Richmond, Va., Union Theological Seminary, 1960. Annotated list; entries alphabetical under subheadings. No index. Some titles in each section marked as "essential."

A Basic Bibliography for Ministers, selected and annotated by the Faculty of Union Theological Seminary, New York. 2nd ed. New York, Union Theological Seminary, 1960. Arranged by fields of Christian studies and literature, following the departmental curriculum (that is, Old Testament, Church History, and so forth) of Union Theological Seminary, New York City. Entries alphabetical in each subject area, with brief annotations to indicate possible usefulness.

A Bibliography of Practical Theology, by the Theological Seminary, Princeton, N. J. Princeton, N. J., Theological Book Agency, 1949. ". . . aim at helpfulness rather than completeness." Two divisions, each in two parts: 1. Homiletics, and Related Subjects; 2. Christian Education, and Related Subjects. Arranged alphabetically under subheadings. Table of contents, but no index.

A Bibliography of Systematic Theology for Theological Students. Princeton, N. J., Princeton Theological Seminary Library, 1949. Alphabetical under 25 headings. Restricted to works written in English. Table of contents, but no index and no annotations.

A World Bibliography of Bibliographies, by Theodore Besterman. 3rd ed. Genève, Switzerland, Societas Bibliographica, c1955. Also, lists bibliographical catalogues, calendars, abstracts, indexes, and the like. Limited to separately published bibliographies. 4 volumes and an index volume. Alphabetical by subject. Cross references.

Bibliographic Index; A Cumulative Bibliography of Bibliographies. 1937- date. (See p. 30.)

The American Historical Association's Guide to Historical Literature, ed. by G. F. Howe, G. C. Boyce, T. R. S. Broughton, and others. New York, Macmillan, 1961. Bibliographical panorama as well as an inventory of the best historical literature extant at the time of compilation, and an excellent means of gaining broader knowledge of history. Arranged in ten sections, each prepared by a specialist; certain sections relate to certain topics, and the remaining ones apply to geographic areas and their peoples. An annotated reference work, with a detailed table of contents and a list of contributors in the front and a full index in the back.

Bibliography of American Literature, comp. by J. N. Blauck. New Haven, Yale University Press, 1955—. In progress. 3 volumes. A selective bibliography, limited to material which constitutes the *structure* of American literature for the past 150 years, from the time of the Revolution. Includes authors who were known and read and who were significant in American literature; those who died after 1930 excluded. Vol. 1—Henry Adams to Donn Byrne; vol. 2—G. W. Cable to Timothy Dwight; vol. 3—Howard Eggleston to Bret Harte. No attempt at evaluation.

Very long preface, list of general references used, list of principal periodicals covered. In the back is a list of initials, pseudonyms, and antonyms.

Bibliographia Philosophica, 1934–1945, ed. by G. A. de Brie. Vol. 1, Bruxellis, Editiones Spectrum, 1950; Vol. 2, Antverpiae, Editiones Spectrum, 1954. Vol. 1—*Bibliographi Historiae Philosophiae.* Strives to list all philosophical literature, books, periodicals, and book reviews published from 1934 to 1945, in Danish, Dutch, English, French, German, Italian, Latin, Norwegian, Portuguese, Spanish, and Swedish. Arranged chronologically according to the lives of the philosophers of different historical periods and schools.

Vol. 2 of the same title—Lists publications treating philosophy in its doctrinal aspects. Classified arrangement. Name index to both volumes. Editorial plans are for a retrospective work every five years.

Religions, Mythologies, Folklores: An Annotated Bibliography, by K. S. Diehl. 2nd ed. New York, Scarecrow Press, 1962. An introduction to the literature of faith and practice in all cultures. Includes books of general and specific references, literatures, literary and historical guides, various scriptures and their commentaries, records of institutional achievement, and biographies.

Table of contents. Each entry numbered, and the index of authors, titles, and subjects refers to these numbers.

Bible Study

Historical Catalogue of the Printed Editions of Holy Scripture in the Library of the British and Foreign Bible Society, comp. by T. H. Darlow and H. F. Moule. London, The Bible House, 1903, 1911. Vol. 1, 1903; vol. 2 (in three volumes), 1911. Confined to *printed* editions of Holy Scripture. Under each language heading *all* editions are arranged chronologically according to dates of publication, showing the history of Bible translation in any tongue. Commentaries omitted unless they contain a continuous text, which is then put under its own language. Vol. I—English, with three-fold index: names of translators, revisers, editors; names of printers, publishers, and so forth, down to 1824; names of places of printing, publication, and so forth, down to 1824. Full description of all early editions. The appendix lists omitted editions.

Vol. II—Polyglots and languages other than English. In three parts (actually volumes): 1. Polyglots; 2. Languages and dialects other than English, alphabetically arranged; 3. Indexes to vol. II, the last part of which is a short index to both volumes, devoted to popular and other names given to certain versions and editions of the Bible, but contains many other entries, some covering vol. I.

The English Bible in America; A Bibliography of Editions of the Bible & the New Testament Published in America 1777–1957, ed. by M. T. Hills. New York, American Bible Society, 1961. "Here one may trace the power of religion and a great religious Book to mold the life and ideas of a nation as it rose from small beginning to greatness." In the front are listed the reference works consulted, as well as location symbols. The index in the back is in two parts—1777 through 1825, 1826 through 1957—annotated, and includes index of publishers and printers, index of translations and of translators and revisers, index of editors and commentators, index of edition titles, and brief general index.

Eleven Years of Bible Bibliography; The Book Lists of the Society for Old Testament Study, 1946–1956, ed. by H. H. Rowley. Indian Hills, Colo., Falcon's Wing Press, c1957. Annotated bibliography, chronologically arranged, then alphabetical. Subject and author indexes. Signed articles; with key to initials (at end of annotations) given in front. Continued by means of a paper-back *Book List* issued annually by the Society, with the same format as the bound volume.

Tools for Bible Study, ed. by B. H. Kelly and D. G. Miller. Richmond, Va., John Knox Press, c1956. Primarily a guide to Biblical study, each chapter by a different author. Goes into detail about the history and use of the particular tool discussed. Each title thoroughly described, with its use and importance analyzed. No index.

Another extremely useful one is *Multipurpose Tools for Bible Study*, by F. W. Danker. St. Louis, Concordia Publishing House, c1960. It intends to bring the student up to date since the publication of *Tools for Bible Study*.

An Introductory Bibliography for the Study of Scripture, by G. S. Glanzman and J. A. Fitzmyer. Westminster, Md., Newman Press, 1961. The list is selective, emphasizing basic titles for the beginner and calling attention to important secondary works. Chapters cover periodicals, introductions to the Biblical texts and ancient versions, lexica, grammars, concordances, and so forth. Full annotations, and for titles under consideration includes references to reviews which have appeared in periodicals. Alphabetical under each chapter, with an index of modern authors in the back, a list of abbreviations in front.

A Bibliography of Bible Study for Theological Students, comp. by staff of Library of Princeton Theological Seminary. Princeton, N. J., The Theological Seminary Library, 1960. Restricted to books in English, except for original texts. Selective and representative, includes points of view of older *and* newer scholarship. Arranged with subheadings under four divisions: Whole Bible, Old Testament, New Testament, and Linguistic Exegesis. Alphabetical under each section; no index.

New Testament Literature; An Annotated Bibliography, ed. by W. N. Lyons and M. M. Parvis. Chicago, University of Chicago Press, c1948. Presents an exhaustive bibliography of books, articles, and book reviews appearing in the New Testament field and related fields, 1943–1945 (with some from 1940 and 1942). Continues series of annual bibliographies for 1940, 1941, 1942. Arranged in sections by subject, each entry numbered. Indexes: author; Greek word and phrase; scripture.

Church History and Missions

A Critical Bibliography of Religion in America, by N. R. Burr, in collaboration with J. W. Smith and A. L. Jamison. Princeton, N. J., Princeton University Press, 1961. 2 volumes (these compose vol. 4 of *Religion in American Life* (see p. 86). Presented in essay form, it provides a general review of the history of religion in the United States and supplies references to illustrate the manifold influences of religion in American life and thought. It is an extensive subject bibliography on all aspects of American religion, with historical and critical notes and titles combined in a continuous narrative text. Full table of contents in each volume, extensive author index at end of second volume.

A Bibliographical Guide to the History of Christianity, comp. by S. J. Case, J. T. McNeill, W. W. Sweet, and others, ed. by J. S. Case. Chicago, University of Chicago Press, c1931. Offers a careful selection of representative titles rather than an exhaustive bibliographical compilation. Arranged by chapters with subdivisions; entries are alphabetical in each grouping. Roughly chronological. Many items are annotated. Key to abbreviations in the front; author index in the back.

The Catholic Church in America; An Historical Bibliography, by E. R. Vollmar. New Brunswick, N. J., The Scarecrow Press, 1956. Composed of a general survey, chiefly biographical; and the bibliography is arranged in a straight alphabet according to main entry. The index is very full and is arranged by subject, location (where), or title.

A Guide to American Catholic History, by J. T. Ellis. Milwaukee, Bruce, c1959. Arranged in sections: 1. Guides, 2. Manuscript depositories, 3. General works, 4. Studies in diocesan, sectional, and parish history, 5. Biographies, correspondence, and memoirs, 6. Religious communities, 7. Education, 8. Special studies, 9. Periodicals, 10. Historical societies. Each entry numbered and referred to by the index. Full author, title, and subject index in back.

American Missionaries in China, by C. H. Chu. Cambridge, Mass., Harvard University Press, 1960. A bibliography of some 7,000 entries of the writings of American missionaries and of Chinese Christians, non-missionary authors, also of some missionaries of Europe, Australia, and elsewhere. Only English books, pamphlets, and articles. Table of contents; index in back is for authors, and in case of corporate entries (see p. 12), the names of organizations are given.

Bibliotheca Missionum, by Robert Streit. Münster i Westfalen, Aachen, Franziskus Xaverius Missionverein Zentrale, 1916–1939. 16 volumes. "Includes voyages, relations, official documents, etc. Gives full bibliographical details, critical estimates, annotations, reference to sources, and in many cases location of copies in European libraries."

Christianity in Japan; A Bibliography of Japanese and Chinese Sources, comp. by Arimichi Ebisawa. Tokyo, International Christian University, 1960. Pt. I—1543–1858. Lists books and manuscripts connected with Christianity which were written in Japan and in China in Japanese and Chinese between 1543 and 1858. Chronologically arranged. In the front are lists of libraries, of sources, of abbreviations for missions functioning in Japan and in China, and a table of Japanese and Chinese era names. Full index in the back.

Bibliography of the Theology of Missions in the Twentieth Century, comp. by G. H. Anderson. New York, Missionary Research Library, 1958. A classified bibliography in four sections: 1. Biblical studies, 2. Historical studies, 3. Christianity and the non-Christian religions, 4. Theory of missions. Some annotations. Alphabetical by author under each section. Covers over 20 periodicals, some foreign. Key to abbreviations in front; two indexes in back —(1) authors; (2) assemblies, committees, conferences, meetings, and so forth.

Source Book and Bibliographical Guide for American Church History, by P. G. Mode. Menasha, Wis., Banta, c1921. "Most significant documents for the entire field of American church history, showing the contributions the church has made to the progress of American society and the manner in which she has adjusted herself to her new and changing environment." The denominational horizon is not emphasized. Restricted to printed materials, excluding newspapers. Annotated. Annotated table of contents; full index in back.

Bibliography of the Continental Reformation: Materials Available in English, by R. H. Bainton. Chicago, American Society of Church History, 1935. To meet the needs of the student of the Reformation who is limited to the

English language. Classified, with some annotations, including books and periodicals. Key to abbreviations of periodicals in front; no index.

Three other useful sources:

Doctoral Dissertations in the Field of Religion, 1940–1952, ed. by E. E. Aubrey and others. New York, Columbia University Press for the Council for Graduate Studies in Religion, in coöperation with the National Council on Religion in Higher Education, c1954.

Doctoral Dissertations in the Field of Religion, 1952–1961, with Lists of Dissertations in Progress. 1962. (Mimeographed.)

A Bibliography of Post-Graduate Masters' Theses in Religion, ed. by N. H. Sonne. Princeton, N. J., American Theological Library Association, Princeton Theological Seminary, 1951.

DICTIONARIES:
THEOLOGICAL, GENERAL

Theological Dictionaries

The Oxford Dictionary of the Christian Church, ed. by F. L. Cross. New York, Oxford University Press, c1958. (Reprinted in 1961, with corrections.) Brings together a large body of information bearing directly on the Christian church, concise and useful, with objective presentation. Historical treatment predominates, including biographies. Alphabetical; extensive cross references and bibliographies. A list of contributors and a list of abbreviations are in the front.

Baker's Dictionary of Theology, ed. by E. F. Harrison, G. W. Bromiley, and C. F. H. Henry. Grand Rapids, Mich., Baker Book House, 1960. A dictionary of theological and ecclesiastical terms, setting forth the meaning of the Biblical content in each. Includes philosophical terms with religious significance, as well as names of various sects and movements which are a part of the history of the church. Alphabetical, with signed articles, cross references, and bibliographies at the end of many articles.

A *Dictionary of English Church History,* ed. by S. L. Ollard, Gordon Cross, and M. F. Bond. New ed. New York, Morehouse, Gorham, c1948. Scope is strictly that of the English church, the provinces of Canterbury and York. Alphabetical, articles signed with initials, brief biographies. In front: list of contributors and their articles, alphabetical list of contributors' initials with full names, list of abbreviations. In back: brief index, mostly *see* references.

Dictionary of All Scriptures and Myths, by G. A. Gaskell. New York, Julian Press, 1960. "Claims to give the true solution of the age-long problem of the origin, nature, and meaning of the Scriptures and myths which are attached to the various religions of the world." Alphabetical, with voluminous cross references.

A Protestant Dictionary, by Vergilius Ferm. New York, Philosophical Library, c1951. A useful tool for quick reference, giving information on terms, doctrines, churches, and movements in a restricted field of interest. Alphabetical, cross references. This is an American publication; there is an English one of the same title, c1933.

A Catholic Dictionary (The Catholic Encyclopaedia Dictionary), ed. by Donald Attwater. 3rd ed. New York, Macmillan, 1961. First was "a simple dictionary of technical words and phrases of the Catholic church"; now is a general work of quick reference to the significant words, terms, names, and phrases in common use in the philosophy, dogmatic and moral theology, liturgy, canon law, institutions, and organization of the Catholic church. Gives, fundamentally, present-day belief, practices, teaching, and opinion; apologetics and historical explanations are secondary. No biographical accounts. Alphabetical, few cross references; useful appendixes in the back.

A Small Liturgical Dictionary, by Cardinal Giacomo Lercaro, ed. by J. B. O'Connell. London, Burns, Oates, c1959. Designed to help the objective of the liturgical movement by giving clear and accurate definitions and explanations of complicated, technical terms. In the front are three sections: 1. The Sacred Liturgy, 2. The Holy Mass, 3. Plan of the Mass, followed by the dictionary, which is alphabetical, with cross references. No index.

Dictionary of Papal Pronouncements, Leo XIII to Pius XII [1878–1957], comp. by Sister M. Claudia. New York, Kenedy, c1958. An attempt to make more readily accessible the directives of the popes. Includes all encyclicals from 1878 through 1957, but only a selection of documents in other categories to June 2, 1957. Alphabetical by title, with cross references from any alternative titles in common use. Title followed by *type* of document, date of writing or delivery, occasion or group addressed, and statement of content. The abstract which follows is not interpretative for essential parts of the text. Has an index of subjects and personal or corporate names.

Concise Dictionary of Judaism, ed. by D. D. Runes. New York, Philosophical Library, c1959. Small, concise dictionary to acquaint the reader with the basic concepts of Judaism in its religious, historical, and cultural aspects.

A Concise Dictionary of Ecclesiastical Terms, by F. L. Eckel, Jr. Boston, Whittemore Associates, c1960. Brief definitions of terms, with illustrative drawings. Based on the Anglican tradition. Slight, but might conceivably be of value to those who are unfamiliar with the vocabulary of the more liturgical churches in reference to parts of the church, various objects used in liturgical worship, and so forth.

A Dictionary of Hymnology, Setting Forth the Origin and History of Christian Hymns for All Ages and Nations, edited by John Julian. New York, Dover, 1957. (Reprinted in two volumes.) Brings together the great mass of historical, biographical, doctrinal, devotional, and ritual matter. Linguistically, the English language is the keynote of this work. Minute technical accuracy. In the front are a list of contributors, a list of manuscripts, and a list of abbreviations. In the back are a cross-reference index to first lines in English, French, German, Greek, Latin, and other languages; an index of authors, translators, editors, and so forth; appendixes of late articles, additions, and corrections. The supplement has an index of first lines and an index of authors and translators. Articles signed with initials. Reprinted in 1960. A revision is now under way, but no projected date has been set for publication. Also in process is a standard work comparable to Julian's dictionary whose title will be A *Dictionary of American Hymnology.*

General Dictionaries

For generations people have either mispronounced words or have used other than preferred pronunciations because they never *hear* otherwise. One person relates the shock he received when he heard someone say Nū'fŭn(d)-land'. He had always said Nū found'land—his geography teacher in grammar school had taught him to say it that way! As a matter of fact, it never was Nū found'land. It looked that way, so his teacher didn't bother to consult the dictionary.

Correct pronunciation is the basis of distinguished spoken language. Those of the clergy who preach, teach, or lecture should certainly be careful of pronunciation, and that includes Biblical names. Otherwise, they lose the full power of communication.

A dictionary gives more information about words than does any other reference book—spelling, pronunciation, meaning, derivation, usage, synonyms, and antonyms. An *abridged* dictionary is condensed. The two most widely used unabridged American dictionaries are *Webster's New International Dictionary* and *Funk and Wagnalls New Standard Dictionary.* When you use a dictionary, remember that in the front is a full explanation of the abbreviations used, as well as a key to pronunciation symbols. The latter is also given at the top or bottom of each page in the modern dictionaries.

AMERICAN

Webster's Third New International Dictionary, ed.-in-chief P. B. Gore, and Merriam-Webster editorial staff. Completely rev. Springfield, Mass., Merriam, c1961. The most reliable American dictionary, with very clear, precise, and sharp definitions given in historical order, with the earliest ascertainable meaning given first for words of many meanings. It is comprehensive, giving coverage of the current vocabulary of standard written and spoken English. It has greatly expanded the technical and scientific vocabulary, not only new terms but new uses of old terms. Alphabetical *letter by letter,* with synonyms of words (if they have such) listed at the ends of definitions.

In the front are very full explanatory notes, an explanatory chart, a guide to pronunciation, forms of address, and abbreviations used in the dictionary. The preface is well worth reading. The dictionary is unabridged.

If you are using the second edition or any of its reprints, you will note that a heavy black line divides each page near the bottom. Below the line are very rare and out-of-date words and long foreign phrases. Above the line are all of the regular words in our language, foreign words, noted names in fiction, and so forth. A number of valuable lists appear in the appendix. Some of them are: (1) abbreviations—the meaning of those in common use, (2) pronouncing biographical dictionary—brief notes about persons, (3) pronouncing gazetteer—brief descriptions of places.

The second edition's reprints have a section in the front called "Addenda" or "New Words," which kept each reprint up to date until the above third edition was published. The second edition and its reprints give synonyms and antonyms.

Funk and Wagnalls New Standard Dictionary, ed.-in-chief I. K. Funk, Calvin Thomas, and F. H. Vizetelly. New York, Funk and Wagnalls, 1958. Another unabridged dictionary. Everything is in one alphabet, except for foreign words and phrases and population statistics, which are listed in the back. A key to pronunciation is at the top of each page. Its emphasis is upon *present-day* meaning, pronunciation, and spelling; for this reason it is the most useful dictionary for quick reference. The *New Standard* gives synonyms and antonyms.

ENGLISH

The Oxford English Dictionary; Being a Corrected Reissue with an Introduction, Supplement, and Bibliography, of A New English Dictionary on Historical Principles . . ., ed. by J. A. H. Murray, Henry Bradley, W. A. Craigie, and others. Oxford, Clarendon Press, 1961. Thirteen volumes. Also called the *Oxford Dictionary.* It is the most scholarly dictionary of the English language, giving the history of every English word from the middle of the twelfth century, with quotations to illustrate its use at different periods.

Nearly everyone has a dictionary at home, most usually an abridged one, and the dictionary is the most "thumbed" book in the library; but many people do not realize how useful it can be if its different parts are known and the "technique" of using it is learned.

See pp. 69–70 for Biblical Dictionaries.

Foreign Dictionaries

Harper's Latin Dictionary, by E. A. Andrews, rev., enl., and in great part rewritten by C. T. Lewis and Charles Short. Cincinnati, American Book Co., 1907.

Heath's Standard French and English Dictionary, ed. by J. E. Mansion, now rev., ed., and comp. with supplement by R. P. L. Ledesert. New York, Heath, 1955.

Theological German Vocabulary, by W. M. Mosse. New York, Macmillan, 1955.

McKay's Modern English-Norwegian and Norwegian-English Dictionary, by Bjarne Berulfsen and Hjørdis Scavenius. New York, David McKay, 1951.

Dutch-English, English-Dutch Dictionary, by J. Cauberghe. 2nd ed. New York, W. S. Heinman, 1962.

McKay's Modern Danish-English, English-Danish Dictionary, by J. J. C. Magnussen, Otto Madsen, and Herman Vinterberg. New York, David McKay, 1954.

Italian-English, English-Italian Dictionary, by Guiseppi Orlandi. New York, W. S. Heinman, 1954.

Spanish and English Dictionary, Diccionario Inglés y Español, by E. B. Williams. New York, Holt, 1955.

ENCYCLOPEDIAS:
THEOLOGICAL, GENERAL

The encyclopedia, like the dictionary, has been used at home or at school by nearly everyone. Most encyclopedias are in a number of volumes and are alphabetically arranged—a term that needs explanation. Some of them are arranged alphabetically by *large subject;* others, by minutely alphabetized small subject. For instance, the *Encyclopaedia Britannica* treats "Anglo-Saxon Literature" as a sub-topic under "English Literature" (Ealiest Times to Chaucer), while the *Encyclopedia Americana* treats it in a separate article, "Anglo-Saxon Literature," in an entirely different volume from "English Literature." The former type, to be of the greatest use, needs an index volume to disclose the location of small subjects.

Before using any encyclopedia, check to see if it is arranged *word by word* or *letter by letter.* (See pp. 9–10.)

Some encyclopedias are kept up to date by the publication of revised editions at intervals of several years. If the interval between editions is long, an occasional supplementary volume is published. Some have a policy of "continuous revision"—in each reprint, some revision is done. Others are kept up to date by yearbooks.

Theological Encyclopedias

Encyclopedia of Religion and Ethics, ed. by James Hastings, J. E. Selbie, and others. New York, Scribner, 1908–1927. This 12-volume set contains articles on all religions, ethical systems and movements, religious beliefs and customs, philosophical ideas, moral practices, and so forth. It is the most comprehensive work in this field and valuable for comparative studies. It is alphabetical, but has a general analytical index, an index to foreign words, an index to scripture passages, and an author index. Signed articles, with full bibliographies. A new edition is in preparation.

New Schaff-Herzog Encyclopedia of Religious Knowledge, ed.-in-chief, S. M. Jackson. Grand Rapids, Mich., Baker Book House, 1949–1950 (originally New York, Funk and Wagnalls, 1908–1912). Another 12-volume set which is one of the most important reference works on the subject in English. Protestant in tone, but unbiased. The bibliographies are excellent. Has an index, cross references.

Supplemented by *Twentieth Century Encyclopedia of Religious Knowledge,* ed.-in-chief, L. A. Loetscher. Grand Rapids, Mich., Baker Book House, 1953–1955. Two volumes, with signed articles, good bibliographies, and cross references.

Encyclopaedia of Religion and Religions, by E. R. Pike. New York, Meridian Books, c1958. A one-volume work with brief articles alphabetically arranged. It has cross references but no bibliographies. The work attempts to present clearly, accurately, and in an unbiased way information on basic principles of natural and revealed religions, on founders and other great personalities, theological tenets, and so forth. Pronunciation list at the end.

An Encyclopedia of Religion, ed. by Vergilius Ferm. New York, Philosophical Library, c1945. A one-volume work on the theologies of the major religions, denominations, and cults. The broad interpretations of religion include its role in labor movements, Negro education, penology, and so forth, and Biblical literature, Christian theology, ecclesiastical history, and many other subjects such as philosophy, ethics, and sociology are treated as well. Alphabetical with cross references, and with bibliographies for long articles, all of which are signed with initials.

The Concise Encyclopaedia of Living Faiths, ed. by R. C. Zaehner. London, Hutchinson, c1959. Deals exclusively with *living faiths;* excludes primitive religions and those of great cultures which have passed away. A survey of the chief faiths of the world, including Marxism, and clearly relates each to the older fields of human belief. Pt. 1—Prophecy, Pt. 2—Wisdom. Excellent scholarship, illustrated. Classified table of contents, giving the author of each section. Full index; bibliography for further reading in back.

CATHOLIC

Catholic Encyclopedia, ed. by C. G. Hebermann, E. A. Pace, C. B. Pallen, and others. New York, Robert Appleton, Index, vol. 16, c1914. 1907–1912. The standard work in English for Catholic history, doctrine, and biography. It is very good for questions on subjects in medieval literature, history, philosophy, art, and so forth. This is an authoritative work with long, signed articles, good bibliographies, and illustrations. In 15 volumes and an index volume. Vol. 17 (1922) and vol. 18 (1950) have been published as supplements.

The New Catholic Encyclopedia, New York, McGraw-Hill. now in preparation, will be published in 1965, as now projected. It will be in 15 volumes, embracing all important knowledge and information having some bearing on or relation to Catholicism and will be of service to the church, the teacher and student, and the general public. It will include cross references, bibliographies, signed articles, and an index volume.

Twentieth Century Encyclopedia of Catholicism, ed.-in-chief, Henri Daniel-Rops. New York, Hawthorn Books, 1957–. In progress—half of the 150 volumes have been published; the completion date has been set at 1965. Each volume in the series is a complete treatment of its subject, with bibliographies and scholarly annotations where necessary. The series is divided into 15 general sub-series on such general topics as belief, faith, the nature of Man, the Bible, and so forth. Individual volumes treat specific aspects of the topics in the sub-series. Vol. 150 will be an index to the other 149 volumes. International in scope.

Enciclopedia Cattolica. Città del Vaticano, Enciclopedia Cattolica, 1948–1954. 12 volumes. An important new work in Italian, largely written by Italian scholars. Concerned with all matters dealing with the Catholic church up to modern times. Signed articles with lengthy bibliographies. A systematic index in vol. 12.

BAPTIST

The Baptist Encyclopedia, ed. by William Cathcart. Philadelphia, Louis H. Everts, 1881. The subtitle reads: A dictionary of the doctrines, ordinances, usages, confessions of faith, sufferings, labors, and successes, and of the general history of the Baptist denomination in all lands. . . . It has numerous sketches of distinguished American and foreign Baptists, and a supplement. Alphabetical, illustrated largely with portraits.

Encyclopedia of Southern Baptists. Nashville, Tenn., Broadman Press, c1958. 2 volumes, paged continuously. "Not an official encyclopedia of Southern Baptists," . . . because of the way Southern Baptists define their policy, but presents "Southern Baptists in the context of their history, their present organization, and their maturing methodology." Alphabetical, cross references, signed articles—many of which have bibliographies. No index.

LUTHERAN

Lutheran Cyclopedia, ed.-in-chief, E. L. Lueker. St. Louis, Concordia Publishing House, 1954. Not restricted to Lutheranism; covers important aspects of the life of the Church since the days of the Apostles, including Biblical interpretation, systematic theology, church history, biography of persons of many denominations (excluding living persons), and life and worship of the church. Alphabetical; some signed articles and some bibliographies.

MENNONITE

The Mennonite Encyclopedia; A Comprehensive Reference Work on the Anabaptist-Mennonite Movement. Hillsboro, Kansas, Mennonite Brethren Publishing House, 1955–1959. 4 volumes. Covers theology, ethics, history, and biography, both historical and contemporary. Articles varying in length, signed, with bibliographies. Very comprehensive. Supplement in vol. 4, also index of illustrations, and maps.

METHODIST

Cyclopedia of Methodism, ed. by Matthew Simpson. Philadelphia, Everts & Stewart, 1878. Embraces sketches of its rise, progress, and condition up to 1878, with illustrations and biographical notices.

PRESBYTERIAN

Encyclopaedia of the Presbyterian Church in the United States of America: Including the Northern and Southern Assemblies. Philadelphia, Presbyterian Publishing Co., 1888. Includes biographies, some of which have a bibliography of subject's writings. Supplement at end. Index shows only subjects and biographies included, no page reference given.

JEWISH

Universal Jewish Encyclopedia, ed. by Isaac Landman. New York, Universal Jewish Encyclopedia, 1939–1944. 10 volumes. An authoritative and popular presentation of Jews and Judaism since the earliest times. Many biographies, including those of living persons. Less scholarly than the *Jewish Encyclopedia,* 1901–1906, but accurate and up to date. Many articles are signed; has some bibliographies. A reading guide and an index are included.

The Encyclopedia of Jewish Knowledge, ed. by Jacob De Haas. New York, Behrman's Jewish Book House, 1938. This one-volume work is a readable guide to Jewish history, incidents, experiences, persecutions, ideas, and cultural efforts and to the lives of great Jews and Jewesses. Alphabetical.

The Standard Jewish Encyclopedia, ed.-in-chief, Cecil Roth. Garden City, N. Y., Doubleday, 1958–1959. This one-volume contemporary encyclopedia has no comparable reference work since before World War II. Special emphasis is on recent historical development (destruction of European Jewry and the establishment of Israel); also covers every phase of Jewish life, literature, and thought from the beginning, prominent Jews from the beginning, and non-Jews who have made major impressions on Jewish history. Concise, has cross references, is alphabetical, but has no index.

Encyclopaedia Judiaca. Berlin, Verlag Eschkol, c1928–1934. Volumes 1–10 (A-Lyra) were published up to the persecution of the Jews in Germany— no more have appeared. Covers all aspects of Jewish life; very scholarly and in German. Signed articles, alphabetical, valuable bibliographies.

ISLAM

The Encyclopaedia of Islam, ed. by Bernard Lewis and others. New ed. London, Luzac, 1960, vol. 1. In progress. A new edition of the 1913–1938 (with supplement 1934–1938) edition, which covers the religion and law, geography, ethnography, and biography of the Muhammadan Peoples. The *Shorter Encyclopaedia of Islam,* ed. by H. A. R. Gibb and J. K. Kramers. Ithaca, Cornell University Press, c1953, based on the above old edition, has up-to-date bibliographies and cross references. Alphabetical, with a subject index.

General Encyclopedias

Encyclopaedia Britannica. Chicago, Encyclopaedia Britannica, 1929– 1956. Twenty-four volumes. Has been considered the most "distinguished" encyclopedia in English, particularly fine in "cultural" fields. The alphabetical arrangement is *letter by letter;* since the information is grouped under large subjects, the index volume is essential for locating small subjects or subdivisions of a large one.

Its long articles are signed with initials, identifiable from the list of contributors in front; good bibliographies and illustrations. Pronunciation is not usually given. The last or 14th edition is more popular in style and treatment than the very scholarly and fine 11th edition and provides some revision in the yearly reprints. The *Britannica Book of the Year,* first published in 1938, is an excellent annual supplement.

Encyclopedia Americana. New York, Americana Corp., 1957. Thirty volumes. An excellent general encyclopedia with emphasis on North America. Alphabetical by *words;* index volume which is necessary for locating small subjects not covered by cross references; many articles signed; bibliographies. Pronunciation is given. Yearly printings provide some revision, and it is kept up to date by the *Americana Annual* (a yearbook).

It formerly gave more attention to applied sciences, technology, business, and government; but recent revisions give more adequate treatment to the arts, the humanities, and the social sciences. Some articles are accompanied by lists of technical terms with their definitions (glossaries). A useful feature is the history and development of each century under the name of the century, as, *Fifteenth Century, Eighteenth Century.*

Collier's Encyclopedia. New York, F. P. Collier, 1957. Twenty volumes. A general encyclopedia with excellent illustrations and many cross references. The articles are signed with initials, which can be identified in the full list of contributors in vol. 1 or in the unit list in the volume used. The twentieth or final volume includes all of the bibliographies and the general index. Kept up to date by *Collier's Year Book.*

Chambers's Encyclopaedia. London, Newnes, c1955. Fifteen volumes. Scholarly encyclopedia with British viewpoint and particularly good scientific articles. Contains excellent bibliographies, illustrations, and text. Alphabetical *letter by letter,* many articles signed with initials. An atlas, an atlas index and gazetteer, a classified list of subjects, and the general index are in the last volume.

For readers of French, German, and Italian, the three following encyclopedias are excellent:

Grand Larousse Encyclopédique. Paris, Librairie Larousse, 1960–. In progress, vol. 4—1961.

Der Grosse Brockhaus. 16th ed. Wiesbaden, Brockhaus, 1952–1957. 12 volumes.

Enciclopedia Italiana di Scienze, Lettere ed Arti. Rome, Instituto della Enciclopedia Italiana (Giovanni Treccani), 1929–1939. Thirty-six volumes. 3 appendix volumes, 1938–1960.

YEARBOOKS, HANDBOOKS, DIRECTORIES: THEOLOGICAL, GENERAL

Among the most useful books in the library are the yearbooks. They are interesting, too, because they contain facts and figures that are within the range of our own experience. Certain yearbooks, general in scope and planned to bring up to date the information covered by general encyclopedias, are published as annual supplements to those encyclopedias. Other yearbooks, that are not supplements to encyclopedias, deal with a special field of interest or with a particular country. Theological yearbooks fall in the "special interest" or "subject" field. Some of them are not necessarily limited to the developments of a single year, especially as to statistics.

Yearbooks are valuable for historical research because they are prepared and published shortly after events occur; they are contemporary with events and reflect contemporary opinion. Almost all of the yearbooks cover events of the *previous* year. Regardless of the date given as part of the title of a yearbook, consult the publication date on the title page or the copyright date on the back of the title page to be sure of the *date* of the material in the book.

A *handbook* is usually thought of as dealing with the subject matter of a profession, a skill, or a technique. *Directories* cover persons, organizations, professions, and so forth.

Theological

YEARBOOKS

Yearbook of American Churches; Information on All Faiths in the U. S. A., currently ed. by B. Y. Landis. New York, National Council of the Churches of Christ in the U.S.A., 1932–date. Now in its 30th issue, and since 1951 has been published annually. Begun in 1916 as *Federal Council Yearbook,* it has changed title several times; present title dates from 1932. Currently it has three sections: Calendar of the Christian Year, Directories, Statistical and historical section. The most complete directory of American Protestant churches, bringing together current, pertinent addresses, statistics, and other useful data, covering the previous year. Table of contents and an index.

The Episcopal Church Annual, ed. by C. P. Morehouse and Margaret Landis. New York, Morehouse-Barlow, 1830–date. The title has changed from time to time. Statistics, diocesan and parochial lists, succession of American bishops, clergy list, list of general organizations. Editorials in front, list of theological schools, classified buyers guide. Not alphabetical, but has a table of contents and an index.

The Official Year-Book of the National Assembly of the Church of England. London, The Church Information Office of the Church Assembly, 1883–date. Presents all types of statistics relating to the Church of England; also has special articles (1961 issue has one on Race Relations). A Who's Who section. Full table of contents and an extensive general index.

The Church of Scotland Year-Book, ed. by J. S. Easton. Edinburgh, Church of Scotland Committee on Publications, 1884–date. Title varies. Includes historical and statistical information and directory information on synods, presbyteries and parishes. Alphabetical list of ministers; index of churches.

The National Catholic Almanac. Patterson, N. J., St. Anthony's Guild, (distributor: Doubleday, Garden City, N. Y.), 1904–date. Covers almost everything pertaining to the Catholic church: News events of Catholic interest during the year, headline articles, calendar information, doctrine of the Catholic church, liturgy and rites, glossary of terms in Catholic use, famous Catholics, and Catholic churches over the world, sports, United States government, and so forth. Not alphabetical; table of contents and very detailed index *in front.*

Year Book of the Evangelical and Reformed Church, ed. by S. E. Mackey. St. Louis, Eden Publishing Co., 1923–1961. Contains statistics for the previous year. A directory of church and lay persons and also statistics. Table of contents (called an index) in front.

United Church of Christ 1962 Year Book. New York, United Church of Christ, 1962–. Contains 1961 statistics from all Congregational Christian Conferences and all Evangelical and Reformed Synods from Jan. 1, 1961 to July 4, 1961, and as acting conferences of the United Church of Christ, July 4, 1961–Dec. 31, 1961. Combines vol. 84 of *The Congregational Year Book,* vol. 90 of *The Christian Annual,* and the *1962 Year Book of the Evangelical and Reformed Church* statistics for 1961. It is the usual directory type of annual. Supersedes *The Yearbook of the Congregational Churches of the United States of America.*

American Jewish Yearbook, ed. by Morris Fine and Milton Himmelfarb. New York, American Jewish Committee, 1899–date. Formerly published in Philadelphia by the Jewish Publication Society of America. Directory, statistical information and special articles, biographies, necrology, and bibliographies. Vol. 40 contains a subject index to special articles in vols. 1–40. Beginning with vol. 44, each volume has an American Jewish bibliography.

HANDBOOKS

World Christian Handbook, ed. by H. W. Coxill and Sir Kenneth Grubb. London, World Dominion Press, 1962. Voluminous statistical tables, lists of ecumenical organizations, national organizations. Alphabetical by country (except Africa); a section on Jewish statistics, and other religions. Full table of contents and a general index.

Handbook of Denominations in the United States, by F. S. Mead. 2nd rev. ed. New York, Abingdon Press, c1961. Brief history of denominations in the United States, with explanation of theological belief, number of members, and so forth. Full table of contents and a full index. In the back are: 1. Alphabetical list of headquarters of denominations, 2. Church membership, 3. Glossary of terms, 4. Bibliography.

The Religious Bodies of America, by F. E. Mayer. 3rd ed. St. Louis, Concordia Publishing House, 1958. Primarily for theological students, parish ministers, and interested laymen. Interprets the doctrines and practices of each religious group in the light of historical development and on the basis of its objective. No statistics, except an appendix in the back on membership by faiths. Bibliography with each section; general bibliography and table of contents in front. Full index.

Churches and Church Membership in the United States, An Enumeration and Analysis by Counties, States and Regions, by the Bureau of Research and Survey. New York, National Council of Churches of Christ in the United States of America, 1956–1958. Covers major faiths and denominational statistics by regions, divisions, or states; denominational statistics by states and countries; denominational statistics by metropolitan areas; and socioeconomic characteristics.

Religious Bodies: 1936, by the U. S. Bureau of the Census. Washington, Government Printing Office, 1941. 3 volumes. (There is also one of the same title for 1926, published in 1930. Both were prepared by the United States Bureau of the Census.) Vol. 1—Summary and detailed tables. Vols. 2–3—Separate denominations: statistics, history, doctrine, organization, and work. These statistics cover membership, church buildings and parsonages, value of and debt on church property, Sunday schools, and expenditures. Limited to continental United States. Reports for 1906, 1916, and 1926 are also available.

The Baptist Handbook. London, Baptist Union, 1860–1956; London, Carey Kingsgate Press, 1957–date. Annual English publication giving directory information on the Baptist Union of Great Britain and Ireland.

The Story of Our Hymns: The Handbook to the Hymnal of the Evangelical and Reformed Church, by Armin Haeussler. St. Louis, Eden Publishing House, 1952. A useful companion to the 561 hymns included in the *Evangelical and Reformed Hymnal,* and useful to other denominations, since hymns are universal in nature and cross all boundaries. Includes helpful articles at the beginning about hymns in general. Main portion of book given over to a discussion of each hymn, with a section of notes and sources. Seven indexes add greatly to the value of the handbook.

The Hymnal 1940 Companion. New York, The Church Pension Fund, c1949. The introduction includes a history of hymnology, a chronological list of texts and tunes, and a brief history of the Hymnal of the Protestant Episcopal Church in the United States. Pt. I covers historical essays on texts and tunes; Pt. II has biographies of authors, translators, composers, and arrangers. Six indexes, including a general index, make the book a useful reference tool.

DIRECTORIES

The Official Catholic Directory, ed. by T. B. Kenedy. New York, Kenedy, 1886–date. Annual. "Useful manual, containing large amounts of detailed directory, institutional, and statistical information about the organization, clergy, churches, missions, schools, religious orders, and so forth, of the Catholic Church in the United States and its possessions, Great Britain and Ireland, Canada and other parts of British America, Cuba and Mexico." Title varies. Brief index in the *front.*

The Catholic Directory. London, Burns, Oates, 1938–1961; Glasgow, Burns, 1962–date. 1838–date. Annual English publication. Gives information on the Roman Catholic hierarchy in Great Britain and Ireland, and on the dioceses of England, Scotland, and Wales. Lists the church dignitaries of the British Commonwealth and the U.S.A.; the priests of Great Britain; religious orders and data on training colleges and societies in England and Wales.

The Clerical Directory of the Protestant Episcopal Church in the U.S. of A. New York, Church Hymnal Corp. for the Church Pension Fund, 1962. Revised every three years. Illustrated. Includes biographical sketches (alphabetical); necrology; deaconesses' biographies; digest of the General Convention; faculties of theological schools; and so forth.

Crockford's Clerical Directory. London, Oxford University Press, 1858–date. (Annual since 1877.) Much statistical and directory information, with largest section giving biographical sketches of Bishops and clergy of the Church of England, and of the Welsh, Scottish Episcopal, Irish, and overseas churches. An essential handbook to the work of the Anglican communion, listing commissions, committees, and so forth, and the members of each. Much miscellaneous information. Includes maps and a good index.

Ministerial Directory of the Presbyterian Church, U. S., 1861–1941; Revised and Supplemented, 1942–1950, comp. by E. C. Scott. Atlanta, Hubbard Printing Co., 1950. Biographical material, alphabetically arranged, of all ordained ministers who have served in the Presbyterian Church in the United States. References made to earlier volume. A list of abbreviations and a brief bibliography in the back. Mimeographed supplement through 1960.

American Synagogue Directory. New York, American Synagogue Directory, 1957–date. Annual. Lists synagogues, with addresses and names of rabbis and presidents of the congregations. Arranged by state and city.

Directory of World Missions, ed. by J. I. Parker. New York, International Missionary Council, 1938. Interpretative survey of the world mission of the Christian Church. Lists missionary boards, societies, colleges, cooperative councils, and other agencies related to the Protestant churches of the world. Detailed statistics, articles, and indexes.

General

ENCYCLOPEDIA SUPPLEMENTS

Americana Annual. New York, Americana Corp., 1923–date. This is the yearly supplement to the *Encyclopedia Americana,* with the same world-wide, general coverage. Excellent record of events of the year previous to publication. Alphabetical by *words,* well illustrated, major articles signed, cross references. Index cumulates every few years to reveal the contents of previous volumes. In the front is a "Chronology of the Year" in two parts: outstanding dates of the year, and a chronological index of the year.

Britannica Book of the Year. Chicago, Encyclopaedia Britannica, 1938–date. Began publication in 1938 to keep the *Encyclopaedia Britannica* always current; covers the previous year. It has the scope of its encyclopaedia, but its presentation is in the dramatic manner of our time, the illustrations typifying the year rather than the editor's viewpoint. Articles are signed with initials; the index is cumulative and is indispensable in locating information not appearing in the *letter-by-letter* alphabetical arrangement. Several feature articles on important topics of the year are found in front; also, a calendar of notable events of the year.

Important material from the yearbooks for 1937–1946 has been assembled into a four-volume work, *10 Eventful Years.*

New International Yearbook. New York, Funk, 1908–date. Originally published as the annual supplement to the *New International Encyclopaedia* (now out of print). General in scope, factual in style, alphabetical *letter by letter,* very few cross references or illustrations, non-cumulative index. Rather brief information, but major articles are signed.

Collier's Encyclopedia Year Book, ed. by W. W. Beardsley. New York, P. F. Collier, 1939–date. Annual supplement to *Collier's Encyclopedia* and a review of national and international events of the previous year. Alphabetical *letter by letter,* signed articles, good illustrations, many *see* references, and a very detailed cumulative index. "Year's Personalities" in the back has biographical sketches.

OTHER

World Almanac, ed. by Harry Hansen. New York, World Telegram and The Sun, 1868–date, and *Information Please Almanac,* planned and supervised by Dan Golenpaul Associates, New York, McGraw-Hill, 1947–date, contain more miscellaneous information than any other reference books. They give recent facts and figures over a wide range of subjects, international in scope, as well as much out-of-the-way data. The *Information Please Almanac* has more general articles (signed) than the *World Almanac,* and its treatment of foreign countries is fuller and more readable. Two of its useful features are the "Headline Stories" of the year and "Chronology" of the year. Neither almanac is alphabetical, but both have good indexes.

A decided advantage of these yearbooks is their "up-to-dateness" accomplished by prompt publication; and they supplement each other.

Annual Register of World Events. . . . London, J. Dodsley, 1758–date. A good review of the year, wide in scope. Not alphabetical; full table of contents and a detailed index. Subtitle has varied during the years.

GEOGRAPHICAL

Yearbooks are published for almost every country, giving the most important facts and figures for the country. It is impossible to list more than a few here, but many others are available.

American Yearbook, ed. by A. B. Hart, William Schuyler, and others. New York, Appleton, 1911–1950. This yearbook has discontinued publication but is eminently useful for the years covered. Good narrative accounts of events and progress during each year in the United States and her territories at that time, and articles on international affairs affecting the United States. Arranged by large subject, with detailed index and table of contents.

Europa Year Book. London, Europa Publications, 1959–date. Supersedes *Europa; The Encyclopedia of Europe,* 1930–1958. A new publication growing out of the trends toward European unity. Pt. 1—European organizations, such as the European Community (including the Common Market); Pt. 2—European countries, arranged alphabetically, giving surveys and statistics. Full table of contents, but no index. Comprehensive and well organized.

International Year Book and Statesmen's Who's Who. London, Burke's Peerage, 1953–date. Excellent annual, published in Britain. Fine articles on timely subjects, varying with each annual; states of the world with pertinent information for each; numerous brief biographies of contemporary statesmen of the world.

Statesman's Year-Book. New York, Macmillan, 1864–date. Statistical and historical annual of the world. Being a British publication, the first part treats the British Commonwealth, international organizations, and the United States, then the other nations of the world. Full index in the back.

South American Handbook. New York, Wilson, 1924–date. A useful guide to the countries of South and Central America, Mexico, and Cuba, with a good general index in the front.

GOVERNMENT PUBLICATIONS

United States Government Organization Manual. Washington, Government Printing Office, 1934–date. Includes the Constitution of the United States, information on all branches of government, with personnel, official duties, and authority. Very useful. Not alphabetical, but has an index of personal names and a detailed subject index.

Statistical Abstract of the United States, by U. S. Bureau of the Census. Washington, Government Printing Office, 1878–date. Standard summary of statistics on the social, political, and economic organization of the United States. Introductory text to each section, source notes below each table of statistics. Annotated table of contents, detailed index. Condensed supplements to the annual abstract are *Historical Statistics of the United States, 1789–1945* (1949) and a continuation to 1952 (1954); also, *Historical Statistics of the United States, Colonial Times to 1957* (1960).

Congressional Quarterly Almanac. Washington, Congressional Quarterly News Features, 1945–date. Readable and popular in treatment, no political bias. Composed of the *Weekly Report* (bills introduced and enacted, committee round-up, floor action, vote charts, week in Congress, Presidential report, and so forth; to this report is published a quarterly cross-reference cumulative index, providing a quick means of relating past events to new action as it occurs) and the *Almanac,* which organizes the past year's material by subject matter instead of chronologically, for permanent reference. Explains how a bill is passed.

This is not published by the United States Government, but it is indispensable for government publications.

POLITICS

Political Handbook of the World. New York, Harper, 1927–date. Designed to furnish the necessary factual background for understanding political events in all countries which have independent governments; colonies and trust territories are not included. Alphabetical by major countries, followed by small or recently independent countries. Table of contents in front, but no index.

UNITED NATIONS PUBLICATIONS

United Nations Statistical Year Book, by United Nations Secretariat, Statistical Office. New York, United Nations Publishing Service, 1948–date. Annual publication of the United Nations Secretariat, Statistical Office. Gives statistics for many areas of importance, including social conditions. Table of contents, introduction, and indexes (subject index, country index) are given in English and in French. Supplemented by a monthly bulletin.

Yearbook of the United Nations. New York, Columbia University Press, 1946/1947–date. Readable coverage of the activities of the United Nations, illustrated with many charts and tables. Pt. 1—The United Nations, political and security questions, economic and social questions, trusteeship system. Pt. 2—Intergovernmental organizations related to the United Nations. Appendixes and a detailed index.

THE BIBLE

Reference Tools for Study

There is no need to discuss here the importance of Bible study in the theological curriculum. However, the quality of work done by a student can be enhanced greatly, and the work can be done with greater facility, if he is familiar with and employs the many reference works dealing with the Bible.

The student will find the following useful in locating translations and editions of the Bible, the texts being too numerous to list here:

The Reader's Adviser and Bookman's Manual, ed. by R. J. Hoffmann. 9th ed. rev. and enl. New York, Bowker, 1961. Up through the 8th ed., 1958, the title was *Bookman's Manual.* The chapter on Bibles is excellent for the beginner.

The Ancestry of Our English Bible: An Account of Manuscripts, Texts, and Versions of the Bible, by I. M. Price, rev. by W. A. Irwin and A. P. Wikgren. 3rd rev. ed. New York, Harper, 1956.

Eleven Years of Bible Bibliography . . ., 1946–1956. (See p. 43.)

The English Bible in America; A Bibliography of Editions of the Bible & the New Testament Published in America 1777–1957. 1961. (See p. 43.)

Historical Catalogue of the Printed Editions of Holy Scripture in the Library of the British and Foreign Bible Society. 1903, 1911. 4 volumes. (See pp. 42–43.)

How Our Bible Came to Us: Its Texts and Versions, by G. G. Herklots. New York, Oxford University Press, 1954.

The Text, Canon, and Principal Versions of the Bible: A Brief Summary of Recent Research Extracted from the Twentieth Century Encyclopedia of Religious Knowledge, by E. E. Flack, B. M. Metzger, and others. Grand Rapids, Mich., Baker Book House, 1956.

Tools for Bible Study. c1956. (See p. 43.)

Multipurpose Tools for Bible Study. 1960. (See p. 43.)

An Introductory Bibliography for the Study of Scripture. 1961. (See pp. 43–44.)

The last three titles above list and evaluate the prime books in the field, serving as a good starting point. Most of the following Bible reference works are described and analyzed in the aforenamed guides.

BIBLICAL LANGUAGE DICTIONARIES AND GRAMMARS

HEBREW:

Grammar of the Hebrew Language, by H. F. W. Gesenius, rev. by E. Kautsch, English tr. by A. E. Cowley. Oxford, Clarendon Press, 1910. Has been called "the best reference grammar in English."

A Hebrew and English Lexicon of the Old Testament, ed. by Francis Brown, S. R. Driver, and C. A. Briggs. New York, Oxford University Press, 1952. A continuation of the older Gesenius-Robinson *Lexicon.*

Lexicon in Veteris Testamenti Libros, by L. H. Koehler and Walter Baumgartner. Leiden, E. J. Brill, 1953. Based on the third edition of Kittel's *Biblia Hebraica.* Words are listed alphabetically and not by root families.

Dictionary and Thesaurus of Hebrew Language, by Eliezer Ben Yehuda. New York, Yoseloff, 1960. 8 vols.

GREEK:

A Greek-English Lexicon of the New Testament, by C. L. W. Grimm, tr. and rev. by J. H. Thayer. New York, American Book Co., 1956 (originally 1889).

A Greek-English Lexicon of the New Testament and Other Early Christian Literature, rev. by W. F. Arndt and F. W. Gingrich. Chicago, University of Chicago Press, 1957. Based on a work in German by Walter Bauer.

A Manual Grammar of the Greek New Testament, by H. E. Dana and J. R. Mantey. New York, Macmillan, 1957.

Theologisches Wörterbuch zum Neuen Testament, ed. by Gerhard Kittell, now ed. by Gerhard Friedrich. Stuttgart, W. Kohlhammer, vol. 1, 1933–. In progress. Not a lexicon, but a vocabulary of New Testament words which in the minds of the editors are theologically significant. A landmark in Biblical study.

A Greek-English Lexicon, by H. G. Liddell and Robert Scott. New ed. rev. by H. Stuart-Jones and Robert McKenzie. Oxford, Clarendon Press. 1925–1940. 2 volumes. New edition. Often considered only as a lexicon of the classics, but useful to the study of the Bible.

A Grammar of the Greek New Testament in the Light of Historical Research, by A. T. Robertson. 2nd ed. New York, Hodder and Stoughton, 1915.

ENCYCLOPEDIAS, DICTIONARIES

Encyclopedia of Bible Life, by M. S. Miller and J. S. Miller. New York, Harper, c1944. For students, ministers, and teachers. Covers the social, religious, and economic background of the early Christian era, arranged under such topics as agriculture, animals, homes, arts and crafts, professions and trades, water supply, and so forth. Each chapter has an introduction with detailed contents listed, and with a full bibliography at the end. Extremely well illustrated with pictures and maps. In the back: maps, with an index; index of Biblical quotations; general index. Also, there is a section called "Date Pegs"—chronologically arranged archaeological and dynastic periods of Biblical history.

Encyclopedia of Biblical Interpretation, A Millenial Anthology, by M. M. Kasher, tr. under editorship of Rabbi Harry Freedman. New York, American Biblical Encyclopedia Society, 1953–. In progress. A massive collection of Jewish interpretations of the Bible, the 4th volume going only to Genesis 36:43. Includes a commentary containing exegetical passages from ancient and modern sources, and an appendix of four essays. Each volume will have at the end: Notes to the commentary, Sources of the commentary, Index.

Catholic Biblical Encyclopedia (Old and New Testament), by J. E. Steinmuller and Kathryn Sullivan. New York, Wagner, 1950–1956. 2 volumes. Covers archaeological, geographical, dogmatic, and biographical sketches. A special chapter on Mariology is added. Gives pronunciation.

International Standard Bible Encyclopedia, ed. by James Orr, J. L. Nuelsen, E. Y. Mullins, and others. Chicago, Howard-Severance, 1930. 5 volumes. In many aspects out of date, but widely used in conservative study.

Encyclopaedia Biblica: A Critical Dictionary of the Literary, Political and Religious History, the Archaeology, Geography and Natural History of the Bible, ed. by T. K. Cheyne and J. S. Black. New York, Black, 1889–1903. 4 volumes. Reprinted with some corrections in 1914. One of the older encyclopedias, but still useful.

Harper's Bible Dictionary, by M. S. Miller and J. L. Miller. 7th ed. New York, Harper, c1961. (Also published in London by Black and known as *Black's Bible Dictionary.*) Incorporates recent discoveries in archaeology, with the necessary changes in dates, geographic chronology, textual criticism, and other current fields of Bible research. New material on Essenes and Gnosticism. Interesting illustrations—maps, diagrams, charts.

A Dictionary of Life in Bible Times, by W. Corswant, completed and il. by Edouard Urech, tr. by Arthur Heathcote. New York, Oxford University Press, 1960. Composed of short articles covering the whole range of life in Bible times. Does not cover such subjects as political history, geography, or questions directly related to theology or literature. At the beginning of the volume is a systematic classification of principal articles in the alphabetical book, under three headings: Secular Life; Religious Life; Animals, Plants, Minerals. Excellent illustrations and a wealth of Biblical references at the end of each article; cross references.

A Dictionary of the Bible, ed. by James Hastings and others. New York, Scribner, 1898–1904. 5 volumes. The standard dictionary of the Bible, containing lengthy articles on places, persons, Biblical theology, ethics, archaeology, ethnology, and so forth. Vol. 5 includes supplementary articles, maps, and indexes. The one-volume *Dictionary of the Bible,* 1947, also edited by Hastings, is an independent work.

Dictionary of Christ and the Gospels, ed. by James Hastings. New York, Scribner, 1907–1909. 2 volumes. "Complements his *Dictionary of the Bible,* but articles written by new authors from new standpoint and with greater range. Designed to give an account of everything relating to Christ in the Bible and world literature, with detailed investigation of the Gospels." Signed articles, with bibliographies. Indexes of subjects and Greek terms.

The Interpreter's Dictionary of the Bible, ed. by G. A. Buttrick, T. S. Kepler, John Knox, and others. Nashville, Tenn., Abingdon-Cokesbury Press, 1962. 4 volumes. Defines and explains every proper name mentioned in the Bible; every major incident; every place, including those in the Apocrypha; every ceremony and rite; every major doctrine and theological concept. Full-length articles on every book of the Bible, on the Apocrypha and other extra-canonical books, including the Dead Sea Scrolls and Gnostic manuscripts, and on the great theological concepts of the Bible.

Well illustrated, full-color Westminster maps, pronunciation given, many cross references and bibliographies.

Seventh-Day Adventist Bible Dictionary, by S. H. Horn. Washington, D. C., Review and Herald, 1961. Presents Biblical and extra-Biblical information concerning individuals, countries, places, objects, and concepts mentioned in the Bible. Illustrated with photographs, drawings, and maps, the latter indexed in the atlas section. Conservative.

The Westminster Dictionary of the Bible, ed. by J. D. Davis, rev. and rewritten by H. S. Gehman. Philadelphia, Westminster Press, c1944. Excellent one-volume dictionary with a good preface, illustrations, and cross references. Pronunciation given. In the front are a list of abbreviations and a pronunciation guide. In the back is a map index followed by maps.

A Companion to the Bible, ed. by Jean-Jacques von Allmen. New York, Oxford University Press, 1958. (Published in England as *Vocabulary of the Bible.*) Not a Bible dictionary, but a dictionary of the major theological ideas and terms found in the Bible. The abundance of cross references makes possible its form of longer articles on fewer subjects rather than a great number of brief articles. Uses the Revised Standard Version for quotations of Scripture. Brief index in the back.

The Bible Companion: A Complete Pictorial and Reference Guide to the People, Places, Events, Background, and Faith of the Bible, ed. by William Neit. New York, McGraw-Hill, 1960. Divisions are: The Background of the Bible, The Holy Land, The Scriptures, The Faith of the Bible, The Social Structure in Biblical Times, The Story of the Bible. Wealth of illustrations; general index.

A Theological Word Book, ed. by Alan Richardson. New York, Macmillan, 1957. Aims to explain a selection of distinctive key words of the Bible as to their theological meanings, based on the English Revised Version of Holy Scripture, with Hebrew and Greek words translated into English. Some entries are very full and others brief; all are signed (some with initials). Alphabetical; some bibliographies and numerous cross references.

COMMENTARIES

International Critical Commentary, ed. by S. R. Driver, Alfred Plummer, and C. A. Briggs. New York, Scribner, 1896–1937. 40 volumes. Commentaries on each book of the Bible, Old and New Testaments, some books combined in one volume, others taking two volumes. Commentaries are by different authors, but some deal with more than one book. In any such series, the quality varies volume to volume; however, this reference work ranks high in the eyes of Biblical scholars—many of the volumes have not been superseded. Especially useful to students and ministers who are not able to read Greek or Hebrew with ease. Each volume has its own index.

The Twentieth Century Bible Commentary, ed. by G. H. Davis, Alan Richardson, and C. L. Wallis. Rev. ed. New York, Harper, c1955. A guide for ministers, teachers, and students in Bible courses, as well as for laymen. It emphasizes the Bible as a whole and points out its theological character and teaching, giving the essential information for understanding the Bible. It comprises introductory articles on the Old and the New Testaments, general articles, commentaries on individual books and verses of the Bible, and a history and analysis of the Apocryphal writings.

Table of contents and list of abbreviations in the front; articles signed at their beginning, bibliographies, then notes on the text verse by verse. Comprehensive index in the back; maps and a map index.

The Interpreter's Bible: The Holy Scriptures in the King James and Revised Standard Versions with General Articles and Introduction, Exegesis, Exposition for Each Book of the Bible, ed. by G. A. Buttrick, W. R. Bowie, Paul Scherer, and others. Nashville, Tenn., Abingdon-Cokesbury Press, 1953–1956. 12 volumes. Long introductions, with bibliographies to the whole Bible, to each Testament, and to each book. Each is written and signed by an individual scholar. The working page is in three parts: at top, the King James Version and the Revised Standard Version in parallel columns; in the center, the Exegesis; at the bottom, the Exposition.

Vol. 12 contains, in addition to commentaries on the last eight books of the Bible, four additional general articles: Transmission of the New Testament, Illustrated History of the Biblical Text, The Dead Sea Scrolls, and Literary Chronology (Old Testament, Apocrypha and Pseudepigrapha, and Old Testament). This volume also includes an index of Scripture cited out of context and an index of subjects.

Abingdon Bible Commentary, ed. by F. C. Eiselen, Edwin Lewis, and D. G. Downey. New York, Abingdon, c1929. Consists of five sections: 1. Articles on the Bible as a whole, 2. Articles on the Old Testament, 3. Commentary on books of the Old Testament, 4. Articles on the New Testament, 5. Commentary on the books of the New Testament. Does not include Apocrypha. Maps and index at the end.

A Catholic Commentary on Holy Scripture, ed. by Dom Bernard Orchard, E. F. Sutcliffe, R. C. Fuller, and Dom Ralph Russell. New York, Nelson, c1953. Based on the current Douay Version but may be used with any other translation, such as the Westminster Version or Msgr. Knox's Version. Critical survey of modern Biblical knowledge, with special emphasis on the doctrinal and spiritual content. Arrangement: 1. Articles of General Introduction, 2. Articles of Introduction to the Old Testament, 3. Commentaries, 4. Articles of Introduction to the New Testament, 5. Commentaries. The Notes for the Reader are important.

Cross references and index references are to section number and letter, not to page number. List of abbreviations and transliterations in front. The author is given at the beginning of each section. Exhaustive index in the back, as well as maps.

Concise Bible Commentary, by W. K. L. Clarke. New York, Macmillan, 1953. Divided into five sections—the first is made up of numerous essays on various aspects of the Bible. The next three take the individual books of the Bible in the usual form of commentary, with an introductory section on each book. The last section is an appendix containing a glossary of Bible words, courses of study, and extra-canonical literature. This work includes the Apocrypha. Full index.

The New Bible Commentary, by Francis Davidson, assisted by A. M. Stibbs and E. F. Kevan. London, Inter-Varsity Fellowship, 1954. Representative of the Reformed approach to exegesis, strongly conservative.

Seventh-Day Adventist Bible Commentary, ed. by F. D. Nichol and others. Washington, D. C., Review and Herald, 1953–1956. 7 vols. Three main sections: general articles, commentary, and supplementary material; verse-by-verse study, maps, full-page sketches of Bible characters. Conservative.

CONCORDANCES

Analytical Concordance to the Bible . . ., by Robert Young. Grand Rapids, Mich., Eerdman's, 1902. 22nd American ed. rev. by W. B. Stevenson, 1902. Part of the subtitle reads "subdivided under the Hebrew and Greek originals, with the literal meaning and pronunciation of each. . . ." Also, "index lexicons to the Old and New Testaments being a guide to parallel passages and a complete list of Scripture proper names showing their modern pronunciation."

The Exhaustive Concordance of the Bible, by James Strong. New York, Abingdon-Cokesbury, c1890. Most complete concordance; provides comparative concordance of the Authorized and Revised Versions and a brief dictionary of the Hebrew and Greek words of the original with references to the English words. Directions and explanations in the front.

A Complete Concordance to the Holy Scriptures of the Old and New Testaments, by Alexander Cruden. New York, Winston, 1930. First edition 1737, reprinted by many publishers in different editions, but no doubt the best-known concordance today. Original edition included the Apocrypha but some editions omit this, which gives it its main value for use today. Not complete, in spite of its title, but because of its simplicity it still has wide use.

Complete Concordance to the Bible (Douay Version), by N. W. Thompson and Raymond Stock. St. Louis, Herder, 1945. *Concordance to the Bible (Douay Version)* was its first title in 1942. This present edition has been much enlarged with many additional words and many added references to words in the first edition.

Nelson's Complete Concordance to the Revised Standard Version, comp. under supervision of J. W. Ellison. New York, Nelson, 1957. Not literally "complete," since some words are omitted ("no," "to," "us," and similar ones) which were not likely to be key words to a passage and which would add to the bulk without adding noticeable value. A complete list of words omitted is found at end of preface. The work for this concordance was done with a Univac I computer; consequently, the context and location of each word could be listed, but not the Hebrew and Greek words from which they were translated.

Harper's Topical Concordance, comp. by C. R. Joy. Rev. and enl. ed. New York, Harper, 1962. (Published in England as *Lutterworth Topical Concordance.* London, Lutterworth, 1961.) Based entirely on the King James Version and not to be confused with the usual concordance. As the title indicates, it enables you to find appropriate texts for a specific topic, even though the topic itself is not among the words of the text. Under each subject or topic the verses appear in their Biblical order.

Alphabetical by topic; abbreviations in the front. No proper names included except those of symbolic significance, such as Babel, Zion, and so forth.

Biblical Subject Index, by W. J. Kiefer. Westminster, Md., Newman Press, 1958. This is actually a concordance, especially for the seminarian and student who cannot afford large Bible concordances. Arranged by subject with subheads and cross references, and with references to chapter and verse.

ATLASES

Atlas of the Classical World, ed. by A. A. M. Van der Heyden and H. H. Scullard. New York, Nelson, c1959. Formerly *Atlas Van de Antieke Wereld.* Has three important features: maps—strictly geographical, plus vividly illustrated aspects of the classical world, including religious, economic, military, literary, artistic, political; series of fine illustrations, many air-photographed, with wide range; text, sketching development of world of Greece and Rome and touching on many cultural as well as political achievements. Full index in the back, also notes on the text.

Atlas of the Early Christian World, by Frederik van der Meer and Christine Mohrmann, tr. and ed. by M. F. Hedlund and H. H. Rowley. New York, Nelson, 1958. The maps reveal in great detail the various parts of the Roman Empire, giving plans of important cities and regions, dioceses, churches, and so forth. The plates show the history of Christianity for the first six centuries. The text discusses the geographical and historical background of Biblical history. Indexes of places and persons, with explanations of the index and of abbreviations used in the index.

Grollenberg's Atlas of the Bible, ed. by L. H. Grollenberg, tr. and ed. by J. M. H. Reid and H. H. Rowley. London, Nelson, 1956. A translation of the 2nd Dutch edition. A scholarly work with an abundance of illustration and a text summarizing Biblical history. A full general index. Fine maps. *Shorter Atlas of the Bible,* by L. H. Grollenberg, tr. by M. F. Hedlund, London, Nelson, 1959, is not a shortened version of the above. It was newly designed to suit the smaller format.

Rand McNally Bible Atlas, by E. G. Kraeling. New York, Rand McNally, c1956. A discussion of geographical references in the Bible. Maps in center of volume. Annotated table of contents; list of color maps and an index of them. In the back is a geographical index, including place names on the maps and in the text, and a subject index. More text than maps.

Westminster Historical Atlas to the Bible, ed. by G. E. Wright and F. V. Filson. Philadelphia, Westminster Press, 1956. Not only an atlas, but a geographical study of the Holy Land in Bible times. Authoritative, with up-to-date maps and articles. In the back are three indexes: 1. To text, 2. To maps, 3. To Arabic names identified with Biblical places in Syria and Palestine. Another useful one is *Historical Atlas of the Holy Land,* ed. by E. G. Kraeling, New York, Rand McNally, 1960.

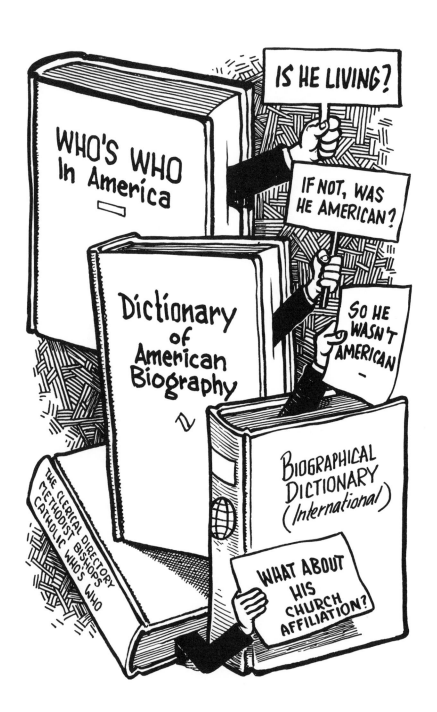

BIOGRAPHY:
THEOLOGICAL, GENERAL

The life stories of famous people are usually interesting, and the books that record them are among the most frequently used in a library. With few exceptions, these books have some kind of limitation. Some are limited to living persons; others, to those who have died. Nationality limitation is common to many of them. Still others include only the outstanding people of one profession. For our purpose here, some are even limited to church affiliation.

Three most important questions that you should ask yourself before looking up a biographical account are: Is the person living or dead? What is his nationality? What is his profession (or his church affiliation)? This procedure will save much time.

Theological Biography

A Dictionary of Christian Biography, Literature, Sects and Doctrines; Being a Continuation of the Dictionary of the Bible, ed. by William Smith and Henry Wace. London, John Murray, 1877–1887. 4 volumes. A biographical dictionary which covers the history of the church from the time of the Apostles to the age of Charlemagne and is a companion to the *Dictionary of Christian Antiquities.* Provides, generally, an adequate account of all persons about whom anything is known connected with the history of the church, of the literature connected with them, and of the controversies relative to doctrine or discipline in which they participated. A standard source with signed articles and bibliographies.

A Dictionary of Christian Biography and Literature to the End of the Sixth Century A. D., with an Account of the Principal Sects and Heresies, ed. by Henry Wace and W. C. Piercy. Boston, Little, Brown, 1911. An abridgment of the above work; does not include the seventh and eighth centuries and does not supersede the above. Some of the original articles have been condensed and brought up to date. Signed articles and bibliographies.

Religious Leaders in America, ed. by J. C. Schwarz. 2nd ed. New York, J. C. Schwarz, c1941. First published as *Who's Who in the Clergy,* c1936. Broad listing of all whose activities are essentially directed to furthering spiritual work. Includes a list of abbreviations, list of divinity schools and theological seminaries, addenda, and biographical sketches, with cross references to the 1936 edition.

Butler's The Lives of the Saints, ed., rev., and supplemented by Herbert Thurston and Donald Attwater. 2nd ed. New York, Kenedy, c1953. 4 volumes, originally published in 12 volumes. This edition is arranged chronologically by the months of the calendar year. The first saint listed each day is the one commemorated in the general calendar of the Western church, if there is one; the rest are treated chronologically, some being entered under day of death (birth unknown). Provides a short, readable account of the principal saints. Cross references at the ends of biographies, some bibliographies, full index in vol. 4.

The Handbook of Biblical Personalities, by G. M. Alexander. Greenwich, Conn., Seabury Press, 1962. A concise, practical handbook which identifies significant personalities in the Bible. Useful to theological students, the clergy, and laymen. It gives the meaning of each name, with the book, chapter and verse where the name appears. Each biographical sketch includes the events of the person's life and his relationship to other Biblical personalities.

Alphabetically arranged. In the front is a section on the meanings of Hebrew names; in the back is a bibliography.

Who's Who in the Bible, comp. and ed. by A. E. Sims and George Dent. New York, Wisdom Library, c1960. A quick-reference tool, especially useful to the beginning seminarian in the identification of Bible personalities. Entries vary in length, but each gives exact Bible references for fuller particulars. Alphabetical. In the front are the following lists: Pronunciation of Biblical names, General notes, The generations of Jesus, The Kings of Judah and Israel. The references are to the Authorized Version unless otherwise indicated.

Dictionary of Catholic Biography, by J. J. Delaney and J. E. Tobin. Garden City, N. Y., Doubleday, c1961. Extensive one-volume reference work on outstanding Catholics from the time of the Apostles to the present time, taken from biographies and historical studies, existing reference works, and so forth; international in scope. Cross references; bibliographies only for major figures. Lists in the back: 1. The saints: As patrons, 2. The saints: Patrons of places, 3. The saints: Symbols in art. Also, a chronological chart of popes and world rulers.

The American Catholic Who's Who, ed. by Walter Romig. Grosse Point,

Mich., Herder, 1911, 1934/1935–date. A biennial work of typical "Who's Who" type of information. List of abbreviations in front; in back are a geographical index, alphabetical by state and then by town, and a necrology.

The Catholic Who's Who, ed. by H. J. Hood. London, Burns, Oates, 1908– date. Slightly irregular in publication. Until 1935 the title was The Catholic Who's Who and Year Book. The 1952 volume is the first published since 1941. Has cross references; contains a necrology and a list of archbishops, bishops, abbots, and priors.

A Dictionary of the Popes, from Peter to Pius XII, comp. and ed. by Donald Attwater. London, Catholic Book Club, 1938. Comprises 258 brief biographies in chronological order, noting the principal events in the life of each of the popes. Alphabetical, with an index of popes.

Popes through the Ages, by J. S. Brusher. Princeton, N. J., Van Nostrand, c1959. Biographical sketches, each one page long, of the line of Roman Pontiffs from Peter to John XXIII, each illustrated with a picture. Chronologically arranged, index in the back.

Who's Who in the Protestant Clergy, comp. by N. E. Nygaard and V. G. Miller. Encino, Calif., Nygaard Associates, 1957. Not comprehensive, since many important names have been omitted. Gives brief biographical and directory information.

Methodist Bishops . . ., by F. DeL. Leete. Nashville, Tenn., Parthenon Press, c1948. Not intended as a complete biographical dictionary of Methodist bishops, but primarily as a bibliography; however, it does contain personal data concerning 250 episcopal leaders of Methodist churches. It is indexed.

Who's Who in Methodism, ed. by E. T. Clark and T. A. Stafford. Chicago, Marquis, 1952. Typical of this type of reference work.

Who's Who in World Jewry: A Biographical Dictionary, ed. by Harry Schneiderman and I. J. Carmin. New York, Who's Who in World Jewry Corp., 1955. Sketches of prominent Jews in various parts of the world, over one-half being from the United States. The U.S.S.R. and her satellites are excluded. The selection of personalities is based exclusively on a record of achievement, except for high officials in government.

General Biography

UNIVERSAL

New Century Cyclopedia of Names. New York, Appleton, c1954. This three-volume set consists solely of information about proper names having importance in the English-speaking world, giving precise and detailed facts. Persons—including mythological and legendary figures—places, literary characters, historical events, and so forth. Alphabetical; pronunciation marked for difficult names.

Chambers's Biographical Dictionary, ed. by William Geddie and J. L. Geddie. New York, Macmillan, 1957. The great of all nations and all times, based on articles in *Chambers's Encyclopaedia*, with hundreds of short articles added. Supplement in front. Pronunciation of difficult names or non-English names. Alphabetical.

Dictionary of Universal Biography of All Ages and All Peoples, ed. by A. M. Hyamson. 2nd ed. New York, Dutton, 1951. Primarily for *identification;* a guide to biographies of prominent men and women, not still living, from earliest history until 1951. Alphabetical.

Universal Pronouncing Dictionary of Biography and Mythology, by Joseph Thomas. 5th ed. Philadelphia, Lippincott, 1930. Includes accounts of famous persons in all countries and of all ages, and of mythological characters. Pronunciation of unusual names.

Webster's Biographical Dictionary. Springfield, Mass., Merriam, 1943. Concise biographies of noteworthy persons of all time. Pronunciation is given detailed attention.

Current Biography; Who's News and Why. New York, Wilson, 1940–date. Universal in scope, giving a biographical sketch of each person, followed by a short bibliography. Numerous pictures. Alphabetical; published *monthly*, with an annual cumulation in December (*Current Biography Yearbook*). The index cumulates back to 1940. The annual volume has a classification by professions and a necrology for the year. Accurate and useful.

International Who's Who. London, Europa Publications, 1935–date. A listing of the world's eminent living personalities. Brief, up-to-date sketches are included, alphabetically arranged. The roster of reigning royal families is an interesting feature. Published annually.

World Biography. New York, Institute for Research in Biography, 1940–date. Annual volume. Affords world-wide coverage; however, references to the United States, Britain, and western Europe predominate. A monthly service keeps it up to date. Alphabetically arranged. Formerly this was called *Biographical Encyclopedia of the World*.

ENGLISH

Dictionary of National Biography, ed. by Leslie Stephen and Sidney Lee. London, Smith, Elder, 1882–1901. Supplements through 1950, the last of which was published in 1959. The best reference work for biographies of famous Englishmen (of Great Britain and her possessions) who are no longer living. Alphabetical arrangement, excellent bibliographies, but no illustrations. When the complete set of 21 volumes was published, its excellence required its being kept up to date, so supplements have been published from time to time through 1950 and will continue to be published. If the person whose life you are searching for is not included in the main set, be sure to consult the supplements.

Who's Who. London, Black, 1849–date. An annual publication about famous living men and women, chiefly English. It gives brief and accurate biographical accounts, including present address. Alphabetical, with no pictures.

Who Was Who. London, Black, 1920–date. A companion to *Who's Who,* containing the biographies of those who died during the period 1897–1916.

AMERICAN

Dictionary of American Biography, ed. by Allen Johnson and Dumas Malone. New York, Scribner, 1928–1937. 20 volumes and an index volume. Two supplements, one published in 1944 (through 1935) and one in 1958 (through 1940). For famous Americans no longer living. Decidedly the best in this field, it is on the same plan as its British counterpart—alphabetical arrangement, excellent bibliographies, no illustrations, and supplements published periodically. The index volume is an analysis of the other 20 volumes, giving among its six sections an index of all *topics* discussed in the set. Another valuable section groups persons according to occupation.

White's Conspectus of American Biography. 2nd ed. New York, J. T. White, 1937. One of the most useful classified lists of Americans who have achieved distinction. It includes, among others, lists of Americans in fiction, poetry, and the drama; pseudonyms and sobriquets; leaders in state and national government, in education, in the arts and sciences, and in the professional fields from colonial times up to 1937. The anniversary calendar is a useful feature.

Who's Who in America. Chicago, Marquis, 1899–date. On the same plan as *Who's Who,* but limited to Americans and published every two years. Occasionally cross references are made to previous volumes. This means that the persons are still living but have no further noteworthy accomplishments that would require reprinting. A geographical index is in the front. Kept up to date by quarterly supplements. Indexes and necrology accompanied the 60th anniversary edition.

Who Was Who in America . . . . Vol. I, 1897–1942; vol. 2, 1943–1950. Chicago, Marquis, 1942–. A companion to *Who's Who in America.*

GERMAN

Neue Deutsche Biographie. Berlin, Dunker und Humblot, 1953–. In progress, 4 volumes having been published. Signed articles and bibliographies; index in each volume. Not intended to supersede *Allgemeine Deutsche Biographie* but has cross references referring to entries in it.

Die Grossen Deutschen, Deutsche Biographie, ed. by Hermann Hempel, Theodor Heuss, and Benno Reifenberg. Berlin, Propyläen-Verlag, 1956–1957. 4 volumes, plus a supplement as vol. 5. Lengthy entries for eminent historical and literary figures in chronological order from the eighth to the twentieth century, illustrated. Vol. 5 includes a cumulative index to the whole set and an author index to vol. 5.

OTHER USEFUL BIOGRAPHICAL WORKS

Twentieth Century Authors, by S. J. Kunitz and Howard Haycraft. New York, Wilson, 1942, first supplement 1955.

American Authors, 1600–1900, ed. by S. J. Kunitz and Howard Haycraft. New York, Wilson, 1938.

Catholic Authors, ed. by Matthew Hoehn. New York, St. Mary's Abbey, 1948–1952. 2 volumes. 1948; vol. 2, 1952.

Directory of American Scholars, ed. by Jaques Cattell. 3rd ed. New York, Bowker, 1957.

Leaders in Education, ed. by Jaques Cattell and E. E. Ross. 3rd ed. Lancaster, Pa., Science Press, 1948.

There is a "Who's Who" for almost every profession of importance and for almost every developed country—far too many to list here, even within the scope of this textbook. Be sure to inquire for such books when needed.

RELIGIOUS HISTORY,
GENERAL HISTORY,
ATLASES

Religious History

The World's Great Religions, by Life Magazine. New York, Time, Inc., 1957. Since few people know anything about religions other than their own, this useful book covers Christianity, Judaism, Hinduism, Buddhism, Chinese Philosophy, and Islam. Clearly and understandably presented, exceptionally well illustrated in color. Naturally, it is a brief survey, with an index.

World Religions; A Brief Guide to the Principal Beliefs and Teachings of the Religions of the World and to the Statistics of Organized Religion, by B. Y. Landis. New York, Dutton, c1957. Concise descriptions of the main religions of the world. Index.

Bibliotheca Symbolica Universalis; The Creeds of Christendom, with a History and Critical Notes, by Philip Schaff. 4th ed., rev. and enl. New York, Harper, 1919. 3 volumes. (Originally published in 1887.) Vol. 1—History of creeds, church by church, with many bibliographical references; vol. 2—Creeds of the Greek and Latin churches, giving for each a full Greek or Latin text and an English translation (in parallel columns), with an index of subjects; vol. 3—Creeds of the Evangelical Protestant churches, in language of the original, with parallel English translation. Index of subjects.

Documents Illustrative of the History of the Church, ed. by B. J. Kidd. New York, Macmillan, 1920–1923. 3 volumes. Selected documents given in translation. Each volume is indexed separately.

Documents of the Christian Church, selected and ed. by Henry Bettenson. New York, Oxford University Press, 1947. Provides illustrations of the development of the Church and her doctrines. Gives a few documents at some length rather than a multitude of briefs. In two parts: Pt. 1—The early church to 451, arranged under doctrinal topics; Pt. 2—From the Council of

Chalcedon to the present, given generally in chronological order. All selections are translated. Two appendixes give a list of councils and a list of books. Indexed.

History of Dogma, by Adolph Harnack, tr. from the 3rd German ed. Boston, Little, Brown, 1899–1900. 7 volumes. (Also New York, Russell and Russell, 1958.) Long considered a "classic"—it is scholarly with numerous footnotes and bibliographies. General index to the set in vol. 7.

The Sources of Catholic Dogma, by H. D. J. Denzinger. St. Louis, Herder, c1957. Translated by R. J. Deferrari from the 30th edition of *Enchiridion Symbolorum.* Presents in chronological order translations of Catholic documents (Papal and otherwise) in which are to be found the bases for Catholic dogma. Goes down to Pius XII. Well indexed, including a systematic index as well as an alphabetical index.

Text-Book of the History of Doctrines, by Reinhold Seeberg, tr. by C. E. Hay. Grand Rapids, Mich., Baker Book House, 1952. 2 volumes in one cover. Vol. 1—History of doctrines in the ancient church; vol. 2—History of doctrines in the middle and early modern ages. Volumes paged and indexed separately.

The Wisdom of the Living Religions, by Joseph Gaer. New York, Dodd, Mead, 1956. Presented in ten parts: Buddhism, Christianity, Confucianism, and so forth, giving the characteristics of each religion. Each part has a statement at the beginning which orients the reader on the religion it represents and makes reference to the sources used. Modern English is used. Contents in front; in back are a selected bibliography, a topical index and a general index.

The Eleven Religions and Their Proverbial Lore, ed. by S. G. Champion. New York, Dutton, c1945. A good comparative study with two indexes; subject-matter index and alternative chief-word index.

Readings in Church History, ed. by C. J. Barry. Westminster, Md., Newman Press, Vol. 1, 1960; vol. 2 to be published in 1963. Vol. 1—From Pentecost to the Protestant Revolt. A ready-reference collection of primary documents for the use of professors and students in seminaries and other educational institutions. Father Barry has included many of the treaties, decrees, addresses, statements, reports, papal bulls, encyclicals, pronouncements, selections from a wide range of economic, political, intellectual, theological, and mystical writings which form the background of ecclesiastical history from Apostolic times to the sixteenth century in this first volume. Annotated table of contents; the index will be in vol. 2.

History of the Expansion of Christianity, by K. S. Latourette. New York, Harper, c1937–1945. 7 volumes. A prime work in the history of missions— the most nearly complete work on the subject now available. Vol. 1—The first five centuries; vol. 2—The thousand years of uncertainty, A.D. 500– A.D. 1500; vol. 3—Three centuries of advance, A.D. 1500–A.D. 1800; vol. 4— The great century, A.D. 1800–A.D. 1914—Europe and the U.S.A.; vol. 5—

The great century in the Americas, Australia, and Africa; vol. 6—The great century in Northern Africa and Asia; vol. 7—Advance through storm, A.D. 1914 and after, with concluding generalizations.

Extensive footnotes and bibliographies in each volume, listing books and periodicals which add greatly to the value of this work. Index in each volume.

A History of Christianity, by K. S. Latourette. London, Eyre & Spottiswoode, 1954. "An attempt to summarize Christianity in all its phases from the immediate background of Christ's life up to the present day. Not a condensation, then, of the author's *History of the Expansion of Christianity,* but a tracing of the development of Christianity in the setting of human history." Selected chapter bibliographies, maps, and a full index.

Christianity in a Revolutionary Age, by K. S. Latourette. New York, Harper, c1958–1962. A 5-volume history of Christianity in the nineteenth and twentieth centuries: Vol. 1—The Nineteenth Century in Europe; Background and the Roman Catholic Phase; vol. 2—The Nineteenth Century in Europe; The Protestant and Eastern Churches; vol. 3—The Nineteenth Century Outside Europe; The Americas, the Pacific, Asia, and Africa; vol. 4—The Twentieth Century in Europe; The Roman Catholic, Protestant, and Eastern Churches; vol. 5—The Twentieth Century Outside Europe.

This recently completed work, adding to the monumental histories already published by one of America's foremost church historians, is the most complete history published to date of the modern period, almost encyclopedic in range. Each volume is indexed and has a bibliography at the end.

Religion in the Twentieth Century, ed. by Vergilius Ferm. New York, Philosophical Library, 1952. A comparative study of religious faiths existing today, in a series of chapters by different authorities. Very readable and adequately indexed. As far as possible, it is arranged chronologically, with a biography of each author and a bibliography for each chapter. Also extremely useful is *Religion in Twentieth Century America,* by H. W. Schneider. Cambridge, Harvard University Press, 1952.

Pictorial History of Protestantism; A Panoramic View of Western Europe and the United States, by Vergilius Ferm. New York, Philosophical Library, c1957. Voluminous and excellent pictures, with running comment, chronologically arranged. Full index.

American Christianity; An Historical Interpretation with Representative Documents, by H. S. Smith, R. T. Handy, and L. A. Lancaster. New York, Scribner, c1960. 2 volumes. Interprets in historical perspective the major movements, both Catholic and Protestant, which emerged in American Christianity between 1607 and 1820 in vol. 1. The development in American Christianity through the middle of the twentieth century is covered in vol. 2. Illustrated; index in back of each volume.

History of Religion in the United States, by C. E. Olmstead. Englewood Cliffs, N. J., Prentice-Hall, 1960. This one-volume survey traces religion from colonial times to the present, set within the broad sweep of political, economic, social, and intellectual history. Brings together many scholarly monographs and treatises on national religious life and thought. Annotated table of contents in front; in back are suggestions for further reading, arranged by chapters of the book. Full index.

Religion in American Life, ed. by J. W. Smith and A. L. Jamison. Princeton, N. J., Princeton University Press, 1961–1963. 4 volumes. Composed of authoritative essays by outstanding scholars, this work is a broad study of the influence of religion in American civilization and of the contributions of America to religious thought. Vol. 1—The Shaping of American Religion, vol. 2—Religious Perspectives in American Culture, vol. 3—Religious Thought and Economic Society: The European Background (to be published in 1963). Vol. 4—in 2 volumes—is *A Critical Bibliography of Religion in America* (see p. 44).

History of the Jews, by Heinrich Graetz. Philadelphia, Hebrew Publishing Co., 1926. (Originally, c1891.) 6 volumes. From earliest times to 1870. A "classic," but would need to be supplemented by more recent works. Indexes in individual volumes. Vol. 6 contains a memoir by Dr. Philip Block, a chronological table of Jewish history, and an index to the whole work.

Jewish Symbols in the Greco-Roman Period, by E. R. Goodenough. New York, Pantheon Press, 1953–. Author's purpose is to try to discover religious attitudes of the Jews in the Greco-Roman world. This monumental work has been described as a "natural history of symbols." Handsomely produced with extensive illustrations; not only a presentation of material, but an interpretative work. Vols. 1–2—Archaeological evidence from Palestine; vol. 3 —illustrations for vols. 1–2; vol. 4—Problem of method; vols. 5–6—Fish, bread, and wine; vols. 7–8 (c1958)—Pagan symbols in Judaism. Each volume well indexed, with lists of abbreviations in all but vol. 3, which has illustrations only.

The Golden Bough; A Study in Magic and Religion, by J. G. Fraser. 3rd ed. New York, Macmillan, 1955. (Originally, 1911.) 12 volumes. A vast store of information about primitive religions, beliefs, and customs, useful in a comparative history of religion. Very detailed index. *Aftermath,* New York, Macmillan, 1956 (originally, 1936), is a supplement to the above work, providing fresh information on certain subjects and some earlier sources not included there. *The New Golden Bough,* c1959, is a one-volume abridgment of the classic work by James G. Fraser. Bibliographies with individual sections; full index of topics, places, and persons.

Mythology of All Races, by W. S. Fox. Boston, Marshall Jones, 1916–1932. 13 volumes. A valuable source of reference material and illustration; the most important in its field. Each section written by a scholar. Extensive and detailed index in vol. 13; fine bibliography.

Mythology; The Age of Fable; The Age of Chivalry; Legends of Charlemagne, by Thomas Bulfinch. New York, Crowell, c1913. Also useful.

Classic Myths in English Literature and in Art; Based Originally on Bul-finch's Age of Fable (1855), Accompanied by an Interpretative and Illus-trated Commentary, by C. M. Gayley. Boston, Ginn, c1911. (New rev. ed. and enl. 1939.) The title is self-explanatory.

Larousse Encyclopedia of Mythology, by Felix Guirand, with introd. by Robert Graves, tr. by Richard Aldington and Delano Ames. New York, Prometheus Press, c1959. Comprehensive, compact biographies of better-known gods, goddesses, heroes, monsters, demons, angels, and saints; uni-versal in scope. Each section or type of mythology written by an authority; classified arrangement. Annotated table of contents, voluminous illustrations. In the back are a selected bibliography, by type of myth, and a very detailed index of names.

Short Dictionary of Mythology, by P. G. Woodcock. New York, Philo-sophical Library, c1953. Alphabetical, with brief explanations, cross refer-ences, no index.

Dictionary of Mysticism, ed. by Frank Gaynor. New York, Philosophical Library, c1953. Brief information, alphabetical, with cross references.

Funk and Wagnalls' Standard Dictionary of Folklore, Mythology and Legend, ed. by Maria Leach and Jerome Fried. New York, Funk and Wag-nalls, 1950–. 2 volumes (vol. 3 in preparation). Deals with the terminology of a special branch of knowledge, a gathering of thousands of pieces of information formerly scattered in manuscripts, journals, monographs, rec-ords of anthropologists, and so forth. Vast coverage. List of contributors in front, with biographies; most articles signed with initials, some with full names. Vol. 3, when published, will contain indexes and a bibliography.

Everyman's Dictionary of Non-Classical Mythology, comp. by Egerton Sykes. New York, Dutton, c1952. "Brief explanations which endeavor to relate myths to the beginnings of history with the hope of fitting them into the puzzle of cultural, historical and religious background." Alpha-betical; classified bibliography in front.

Dictionary of Mythology, Folklore and Symbols, by Gertrude Jobes. New York, Scarecrow Press, 1961. 2 volumes. Useful in showing that people have a common or related background, that symbols and symbolic situations of legends and myths unite all peoples. Alphabetical, no cross references, ex-tensive bibliography in back.

Curiosities of Popular Customs and of Rites, Ceremonies, Observances, and Miscellaneous Antiquities, comp. by W. S. Walsh. Philadelphia, Lippin-cott, c1925. (Originally, 1897.) Origins of holidays, rites, and so forth, par-ticularly those relating to religion. A compilation of strange, out-of-the-way items not usually covered in other reference books. Alphabetical, some cross references, some sources listed. No index.

Days and Customs of All Faiths, by H. V. Harper. New York, Fleet Pub-lishing Co., c1957. The book is exactly what the title claims, containing a wealth of information many people want, interesting and informative facts which enrich the teaching ministry. Pt. 1—Table of contents; arrangement of text is chronological by months of the year, then by day. Pt. 2—Customs (some Jewish terms and traditions, some holiday customs, words and expressions, wedding customs).

American Book of Days, by G. W. Douglas, rev. by H. D. Compton. New York, Wilson, c1948. Contains information about holidays, festivals, notable anniversaries, holy days, giving their history and the customs of celebrating them here and in other countries. Chronologically arranged, with a full index.

General History

The Cambridge Ancient History, ed. by S. A. Cook, J. B. Bury, F. E. Adcock, and others. Cambridge, University Press, 1923–1939. 12 volumes, 5 volumes of plates. Excellent reference work, each chapter written by a specialist, with full bibliographies at end of each volume. New editions of vols. 1 and 2 in preparation.

The Cambridge Mediaeval History, planned by J. B. Bury, ed. by H. M. Gwatkin and J. P. Whitney. New York, Macmillan, 1911–1936. 8 volumes, and maps. Authoritative work on the history of the mediaeval world. As in the above work, each chapter is written by an authority. Full bibliography with each chapter.

The Cambridge Modern History, planned by Lord Acton, ed. by A. W. Ward, G. W. Prothero, and Stanley Leathes. New York, Macmillan, 1934. (Originally, 1902–1912.) 13 volumes and atlas. "The most important general modern history, useful for reference purposes because of its high authority." Lengthy bibliographies with each chapter; detailed general index and miscellaneous tables in the index volume.

The New Cambridge Modern History, ed. by G. R. Potter, J. O. Lindsey, J. P. T. Bury, and others. Cambridge, University Press, 1957–. In progress. "An entirely new work, altogether similar in scope and structure to the original edition. Scholarly reviews of the volumes published thus far find them generally disappointing." No bibliographies and few footnotes; so for reference purposes, the earlier edition should be in the library collection. Vol. 14 will contain a "Companion to Modern History" and an atlas.

New Larned History for Ready Reference, Reading and Research, by J. N. Larned; new, rev. ed. by D. E. Smith. Springfield, Mass., Nichols, 1922. 1922–1924. 12 volumes. Universal in scope, this reference work presents the actual words of authorities whose works are quoted, giving exact references to sources. Includes biographical material and is illustrated. Alphabetical.

Encyclopedia of World History, ed. by W. L. Langer. Rev. ed. Boston, Houghton, 1952. A chronological outline of historical facts covering ancient, medieval, and modern history through 1950. Emphasizes political, military, and diplomatic history. In the back is a list of events from January 1, 1951 to April 30, 1952. Very exhaustive index in the back; illustrated, cross references. Useful appendix.

Dictionary of European History, by W. S. Roeder, introd. by H. E. Barnes. New York, Philosophical Library, c1954. Concise, reliable information concerning most of the events and prominent personalities from 500 A.D. in European history. Brief articles, alphabetically arranged.

OTHER USEFUL REFERENCE WORKS IN THE FIELD OF HISTORY

Album of American History, ed. by J. T. Adams, R. V. Coleman, and W. J. Burke. New York, Sarib, 1944–1949. 5 vols.

Pageant of America, ed. by R. H. Gabriel. New Haven, Yale University Press, 1925–1929. 15 vols.

Dictionary of American History, ed. by J. T. Adams. 2nd rev. ed. New York, Scribner, 1942. 5 vols.

New Dictionary of American History, by Michael Martin and Leonard Gelber. New York, Philosophical Library, 1952.

Encyclopedia of American History, by R. B. Morris. New York, Harper, c1953.

10 Eventful Years, ed. by Walter Yust. Chicago, Encyclopaedia Britannica, 1947.

Historical Abstracts, 1775–1945, ed. by E. H. Boehm. New York, Historisches Seminary, 1955–.

Historic Notebook, comp. by E. C. Brewer. Philadelphia, Lippincott, 1911.

Handbook of Universal History, by G. P. Putnam. New York, Putnam, 1927.

Ploetz' Epitome of History, by J. K. Ploetz, tr. by W. H. Tillinghast, rev. by H. E. Barnes and others. New York, Blue Ribbon Books, 1925.

An Encyclopedia of Latin-American History, by M. R. Martin and G. H. Lovett. New York, Abelard-Schuman, c1956.

Atlases

Historical Atlas, by W. R. Shepherd. 8th ed. New York, Barnes & Noble, 1956. The best of the small, general historical atlases, covering the period 1450 B.C.–1929 A.D., with a supplement of historical maps since 1929. The full index in the back indicates when an entry is a geographical feature other than a town or city. Read the statement at the beginning of the index to understand exactly how to use the atlas. *Atlas of World History*, ed. by R. R. Palmer, Knight Biggerstaff, and others, New York, Rand McNally, 1957, is another useful one.

Atlas of American History, ed.-in-chief, J. T. Adams. New York, Scribner, 1943. Contains the geographical history of the United States, arranged by date from the voyages of discovery to 1912. Supplements the *Dictionary of American History*. Another useful one is the *Historical Atlas of the United States*, by C. L. Lord and H. E. Lord. Rev. ed. New York, Holt, 1953.

Life Pictorial Atlas of the World, by the eds. of *Life* and Rand McNally. New York, Time, Inc., 1961. Uses two kinds of reference maps—terrain maps (three-dimensional simulation of land forms and the earth's vegetation), and political maps (place names). Fine maps, excellent color photographs, charts, text, statistics, and a full index in the back. An exciting new kind of atlas.

Prentice-Hall's World Atlas. Englewood Cliffs, N. J., Prentice-Hall, 1958. Beautifully executed maps, with an index.

Rand McNally Commercial Atlas and Marketing Guide. 93rd ed. New York, Rand McNally, 1962. In two parts: the United States and possessions; the World. Each map is followed by a full index. For the second part, a full foreign index is included in the back. Numerous supplementary tables are given. Another fine atlas is the *International World Atlas*, New York, Rand McNally, c1961. *Hammond's Ambassador World Atlas*, Maplewood, N. J., C. S. Hammond, c1961, has space maps and one of its world maps is for major religions of the world. Other useful ones published by Hammond, c1961, are *Universal World Atlas* and *Standard World Atlas*.

Times Atlas of the World. London, London Times Publishing Co., 1955–1960. 5 volumes. More extensive than any other atlas; good maps.

Some other useful atlases are:

Caxton World Atlas, ed. by W. G. East. London, Caxton, c1960.

Cosmopolitan World Atlas. Rev. and enl. ed. New York, Rand McNally, 1959.

Encyclopaedia Britannica World Atlas. Chicago, Encyclopaedia Britannica, 1951.

For Bible atlases, see p. 74.

There is no doubt that by the time this book comes off the press, there will be new editions of many of the above atlases, so be sure to get the most recent edition.

Along with atlases, some geographical reference books or those which contain much geographical information will prove helpful, especially as to descriptive material and pronunciation.

Columbia Lippincott Gazetteer of the World, ed. by L. E. Seltzer. New York, Columbia University Press, 1952. A gazetteer is a geographical dictionary. This one covers every type of geographical location and feature in the world. Gives pronunciation of each, as well as important information. 1950 census figures. Many cross references.

Much geographical information is found in the *World Almanac* and also in Ayer's *Directory of Newspapers and Periodicals*, Philadelphia, Ayer, 1880–date, which is published annually and covers Canada, the United States, and the West Indies, with maps. *The Columbia Encyclopedia*, ed. by William Bridgwater and E. J. Sherwood, 2nd rev. ed., New York, Columbia University Press, 1956 (Supplement, *Record of Events, 1950–1959*, c1959), and the *Century Cyclopedia of Names*, ed. by B. E. Smith, rev. and enl., New York, Century, c1914, are useful for identification of geographical names.

Webster's Geographical Dictionary. Rev. ed. Springfield, Mass., Merriam, 1955. Gives names of places with geographical information and pronunciation, population figures for 1950, numerous maps.

LITERATURE:
THEOLOGICAL, GENERAL

Primary to the study of many areas of theology, liturgics, and the history of Biblical criticism are the writings by early Christian authors known as "The Church Fathers" or "The Fathers of the Church." The principal source of these writings in collection has been the *Patrologiae Cursus Completus Seu Bibliotheca Universalis . . . Series Latina 1844–1880* (221 volumes) and *Series Graeca 1857–1866* (166 volumes), edited by Jacques Paul Migne and commonly referred to as the "Migne." *Corpus Christianorum*, Turnholti, Typographi Brepols, 1953–, is a modern edition which is of major importance, since it is intended to replace the Migne and to become the definitive critical text. Only a dozen or so volumes have appeared. However, for the beginning theological student whose grasp of Latin and Greek may not be so facile, there are translations of many of the important works in this body of material.

One of the oldest collected translations is the following series:

Ante-Nicene Fathers; Translation of the Writings of the Fathers Down to A.D. 325, ed. by Alexander Roberts and James Donaldson. American reprint of the Edinburgh edition, revised and chronologically arranged with brief prefaces and occasional notes, by A. C. Coxe. Grand Rapids, Mich., Eerdmans, 1950–1951. 10 volumes, plus bibliography and index volume.

A Select Library of Nicene and Post-Nicene Fathers of the Christian Church, ed. by Philip Schaff and others. Grand Rapids, Mich., Eerdmans (originally, 1886–1889). First series, 1956, 14 volumes. Second series, tr. under supervision of Philip Schaff and Henry Wace, 1952–1956, 14 volumes (originally issued 1896–1897). First series consists of works of Augustine and Chrysostom. Second series is, in a general sense, a history of or historical commentary on the first three centuries of the Christian Church. Notes to the text contain much supplementary information as to persons, places, and events. References to authorities and sources are very full. Not alphabetical, but each volume has various indexes; and the last volume has indexes of authors, names, words and phrases, places, and subjects.

Newer series which contain various selections are:

Ancient Christian Writers; The Works of the Fathers in Translation. Westminster, Md., Newman Press, 1946–date. In progress; some 30 volumes already in print.

The Fathers of the Church; A New Translation. New York, Fathers of the Church, Inc., 1947–date. In progress; about 41 volumes to date.

Library of Christian Classics. Philadelphia, Westminster Press, 1953–date. Also in progress; about 24 volumes available. Critical introductions and texts.

Sources Chrétiennes, ed. by H. de Lubac and J. K. Daniélou. Paris, Éditiones du Cerf, 1941–date. Latin or Greek text with commentary in French.

OTHER SOURCES OF RELIGIOUS LITERATURE

Home Book of Bible Quotations, ed. by B. E. Stevenson. New York, Harper, 1949. Based on the King James Version, with a few references to variations in the Revised Version, including the Apocrypha. Quotations and summaries of famous Bible stories are given. Exact citation is given to the book, chapter, and verse. The book itself and the table of contents are arranged by subject. It is thoroughly indexed, not only for page but for location on the page. Many cross references.

The Book of Catholic Quotations, selected and ed. by John Chapin. New York, Farrar, Straus, and Cudahy, c1956. "Entirely from the Catholic viewpoint. Comprehensive work, general in scope, in which specifically Catholic element is allowed to play its proper part. For the lay or average reader and for the specialist. Largely confined to Catholic sources from English-speaking world, with the exception of the supreme pontiffs and the Code of Canon Law." Alphabetical by broad subject, detailed subject and author indexes.

A Treasury of Jewish Quotations, ed. by J. L. Baron. New York, Crown, 1956. "The first attempt at an all-inclusive compilation covering the entire range of Jewish history and thought in all ages, in all lands, and all tongues." Classified arrangement, then alphabetical under each topic. An author index and a subject index, bibliography, and a glossary, "Jewish thoughts from Biblical days to present times."

The Vocabulary of the Church; A Pronunciation Guide, by R. C. White. New York, Macmillan, 1960. A guide to the pronunciation of the language of the church, edited in the light of current professional usage. Includes many proper names of current importance and all Biblical person and place names in their variant forms, other Biblical words of importance, person and place names important to the history, ecclesiology, and doctrines of the church, and the "jargon" of Christianity. Pronunciation instructions given in the introduction, with key at bottom of each page. Alphabetically arranged.

General Literature

Oxford Classical Dictionary, ed. by Max Cary, H. J. Rose, H. P. Harvey, and others. New York, Oxford University Press, 1949. Covers biography, literature, philosophy, religion, mythology, science, geography, and so forth. Most entries are treated briefly, but there are some longer survey articles. A scholarly dictionary with signed articles, most of which have bibliographies, it includes English and foreign works. Pronunciation not given.

ENGLISH AND EUROPEAN

Cambridge History of English Literature, ed. by A. W. Ward and A. R. Waller. New York, Columbia University Press, 1907–1927. The most important history of English literature, in 15 volumes, arranged by periods from earliest times through the nineteenth century. Excellent bibliographies and an index are in the back of each volume. The general index is for the English edition; it is useful only to indicate volumes in the American edition. This indication is sufficient, however, since page references can be located easily through the index in the designated volume.

Oxford History of English Literature, ed. by F. P. Wilson and Bonamy Dobrée. New York, Oxford University Press, 1945–1959–. To be completed in 12 volumes, with each being prepared by a different authority; an excellent reference work. It embodies the latest results of scholarship. The general pattern of each volume has in the back a chronological table, an extensive bibliography, and an index.

A Literary History of England, ed. by A. C. Baugh. New York, Appleton-Century-Crofts, c1948. One-volume history of the literature of England, from earliest times through 1939. Chronologically arranged, with a very full index.

New Century Handbook of English Literature, ed. by C. L. Barnhart and W. D. Halsey. New York, Appleton-Century-Crofts, 1956. Useful reference tool for identifying English writers, works of literature, characters in literature, and various related items. Includes, also, great Irish writers and those classified as Anglo-American, Canadian, Australian, and South African. Alphabetical, pronunciation given, cross references.

Dictionary of Anonymous and Pseudonymous English Literature, by Samuel Halkett and John Laing. Vols. 1–7 new and enl. ed. by James Kennedy, W. A. Smith, and A. F. Johnson. Edinburgh, Oliver and Boyd, 1926–1934. Vol. 8 by D. E. Rhodes and A. E. C. Simoni. Edinburgh, Oliver and Boyd, 1956. 1926–1956. 8 volumes. Vol. 6 includes a supplement; vol. 7, indexes and 2nd supplement; vol. 8 covers 1900–1950. A comprehensive list arranged alphabetically by first word of the title, not an article, giving title, size, place, date, paging, author's name, authorities for attribution of authorship.

Oxford Companion to English Literature, by Paul Harvey. 3rd ed. New York, Oxford University Press, 1946. A reader's handbook for English literature, doing for one literature what Benét does for world literature.

Columbia Dictionary of Modern European Literature, ed. by Horatio Smith and others. New York, Columbia University Press, 1947. Broad in scope, covering the literatures of continental Europe in the twentieth century and the immediately preceding decades. Biographical sketches of the writers, alphabetical articles signed with initials, and short, chronological bibliographies are included.

AMERICAN

Cambridge History of American Literature, ed. by W. P. Trent and others. New York, Putnam, 1917–1921. This four-volume work does for American literature what the above Cambridge history does for English literature. It covers not only the ordinary literary forms and subjects and standard writers, but also early travelers' accounts, colonial newspapers, children's literature, and non-English writings.

The arrangement is: vol. 1—Colonial and Revolutionary Literature; vol. 2—Early National Literature; vols. 3 and 4—Later National Literature. Very full, important bibliographies, arranged by chapter, are at the ends of vols. 1, 2, and 4 with the author, title, and subject index.

The 1943 edition of three volumes in one, New York, Macmillan, 1933, each with its own annotated table of contents and index, is extremely useful for less scholarly purposes. The extensive bibliographies are omitted from this edition.

Literary History of the United States, ed. by R. E. Spiller and others. New York, Macmillan, 1948. Supplements the *Cambridge History of American Literature* for modern American writings and offers some contemporary opinions of the contents of the *Cambridge History.* Chapters are arranged chronologically through 1946, each one an essay by an authority. It appears in three volumes; the final volume is a comprehensive bibliography with an index.

The 1953 edition is two volumes in one, with a "Postscript at Mid-Century" added to cover 1948–1953. The bibliography chapter is for the general reader.

Oxford Companion to American Literature, by J. D. Hart. 3rd ed. New York, Oxford University Press, 1956. Has much the same scope for American literature as the *Oxford Companion to English Literature* has for England but is fuller. Includes a chronological index in parallel columns, giving the literary and social history of America from 1000 to 1955. Alphabetical.

Another in this field is *American Authors and Books, 1640–1940,* ed. by W. J. Burke and W. D. Howe. New York, Crown, 1943.

A *Dictionary of American-English Usage* . . ., by Margaret Nicholson. New York, Oxford University Press, 1957. A simplified adaptation of Fowler's *Modern English Usage,* with American variations. Alphabetical; a list of abbreviations in front and also a key to pronunciation and a "List of General Articles." Cross references.

Webster's Dictionary of Synonyms. Springfield, Mass., Merriam, 1942. Comprehensive for synonyms, also including antonyms and lists of analogous words and their opposites. Words of like meaning are distinguished from each other by careful discrimination and illustration from classical contemporary writers. Includes an introduction on the history of synonymy.

SOME OTHER USEFUL REFERENCE BOOKS IN THE FIELD OF LITERATURE

Warner Libary of the World's Best Literature, ed. by J. W. Cunliffe. New York, Warner Library, 1917.

Cassell's Encyclopedia of World Literature, ed. by S. H. Steinberg. New York, Funk, c1954. 2 vols.

Encyclopedia of Literature, ed. by J. T. Shipley. New York, Philosophical Library, c1946.

Reader's Encyclopedia, ed. by W. R. Benét. New York, Crowell, c1955.

Dictionary of World Literature, by J. T. Shipley. New York, Philosophical Library, 1953.

Oxford Companion to Classical Literature, comp. and ed. by Sir Paul Harvey. Oxford, Clarendon Press, [1959].

Oxford Companion to French Literature, comp. and ed. by Sir Paul Harvey and J. E. Heseltine. Oxford, Clarendon Press, 1959.

Handbook to Literature, by W. F. Thrall and Addison Hibbard. Rev. and enl. by C. H. Holman. New York, Odyssey Press, c1960.

Home Book of Verse, by B. E. Stevenson. 9th ed. New York, Holt, 1953, and *Home Book of Modern Verse,* by B. E. Stevenson. New York, Holt, 1953.

Home Book of Quotations, by B. E. Stevenson. New York, Dodd, 1959.

Familiar Quotations, by John Bartlett. 13th ed. completely rev. Boston, Little, Brown, c1955.

New Cyclopedia of Practical Quotations, ed. by J. K. Hoyt, comp. by K. L. Roberts. New York, Funk, 1947.

FPA Book of Quotations, ed. by F. P. Adams. New York, Funk, c1952.

Oxford Dictionary of Quotations, 2nd ed. New York, Oxford University Press, 1953.

The Best American Short Stories . . . *and the Yearbook of the American Short Story,* ed. by E. J. O'Brien, Martha Foley, and others. Boston, Houghton, 1915–date.

The Best Plays of. . . . New York, Dodd-Mead, 1894/1899–date. (Title and editors vary.)

Funk and Wagnalls Standard Handbook of Synonyms, Antonyms and Prepositions, by J. C. Ferald, rev. and rewritten by Funk and Wagnalls ed. staff. New York, Funk and Wagnalls, 1947.

PHILOSOPHY, PSYCHOLOGY, SOCIOLOGY, EDUCATION

Philosophy

A History of Philosophy, by Frederick Copleston. New rev. ed. Westminster, Md., Newman Press, 1946–1959. 5 volumes. "A lucid and scholarly work, written from the standpoint of the scholastic philosopher, and the only recent extensive history of philosophy in English." General index and bibliography in vol. 1; two indexes (names, subjects) and a bibliography in vol. 2; in vols. 3, 4, and 5, a general index and a bibliography. Annotated table of contents in each volume.

Masterpieces of World Philosophy, in Summary Form, ed. by F. N. McGill and I. P. McGreal. New York, Salem Press, c1961. 2 volumes. Compact summaries in essay-reviews of philosophical works, beginning with fragments from the teachings of Anaximander and tracing the course of man's thoughts down to the present day. Each essay-review is preceded by the name and dates of the author of the original work, when transcribed, and principal ideas advanced.

Authoritative reference work, chronologically arranged by date of publication. Alphabetical list of titles in front; author index in back.

Enciclopedia Filosofica. Rome, Instituto per la Collaborazione Culturale, c1957. 4 volumes. A scholarly Italian encyclopedia with signed articles and bibliographies. Treats philosophical concepts and schools and relevant matters in literature, science, law, and so forth. Many biographical articles. At the end of vol. 4 are three indexes: 1. Classified by theoretical concept, 2. Classified by historical development, 3. Analytical index of terms and personal names referred to in the text but not used as entries.

The Concise Encyclopaedia of Western Philosophy and Philosophers, by J. O. Urmson. London, Hutchinson, c1960. Alphabetical and illustrated. In the back are notes on the contributors and an extensive bibliography for further reading. *Bold type* within an article denotes a separate entry on the person or philosophical term which should be referred to for further cross reference.

Dictionary of Scholastic Philosophy, by Bernard Wuellner. Milwaukee, Bruce, c1956. Primarily for the undergraduate and the beginner who need an understanding of terms. Brief; gives usage as part of speech, with the recognition that only context can give full meaning of a word. Alphabetical; has cross references, a guide to abbreviations, and a bibliography.

A Dictionary of Philosophy in the Words of Philosophers, ed. by J. R. Thompson. London, R. D. Dickinson, 1887. Taken from writers of the times and from books in English, including translations of classical works. Not alphabetical, but in the back is an index of names and a subject index. Full bibliography of works quoted is in the front.

Dictionary of Philosophy and Psychology, by J. M. Baldwin. New York, Macmillan, 1901–1905. 3 volumes in 4. (Reprint: New York, Peter Smith, 1940.) Old but excellent for background. Includes many of the principal concepts of ethics, logic, aesthetics, philosophy of religion, mental pathology, anthropology, biology, neurology, physiology, economics, political and social philosophy, and so forth, giving terminology in English, French, German, and Italian. Illustrated.

The New Dictionary of Psychology, by P. L. Harriman. New York, Philosophical Library, c1947. Brief definitions and biographical notes.

A Dictionary of Pastoral Psychology, by Vergilius Ferm. New York, Philosophical Library, c1955. Selections from the general field of psychology— items of interest which have some relevance to the minister's own use of such material. Also included are topics of a practical nature—visitation, counseling, sermon preparation, preaching, and so forth, as well as entries of a homiletical, philosophical, and exhortative nature. Some long passages, such as Pastoral counseling and case studies, Religion and mental health. Alphabetical; cross references.

Sociology

Encyclopaedia of the Social Sciences, ed.-in-chief, E. R. A. Seligman, associate editor, Alvin Johnson. New York, Macmillan, 1930–1935. This 15-volume work is the only one covering all of the social sciences. It is international in scope and very readable. Its articles are written and signed by specialists; a large proportion are biographies. Its bibliographies and cross references are excellent. Alphabetical; the last volume has a general index whose use is necessary for locating much material that does not appear as entries in the alphabetical arrangement. A reprint edition, 1948, has eight volumes (2 in 1), but the index indicates volume numbers in the 15-volume set.

Dictionary of Social Science, by J. T. Zadrozny, introd. by W. F. Ogburn. Washington, D. C., Public Affairs Press, c1959. "Fills the need for a dictionary of social science terms because of the infiltration of these terms into the common language with inadequate definitions in the usual dictionary." Helps communication for the specialist and the layman. Alphabetical, with cross references.

Dictionary of Sociology, ed. by H. P. Fairchild. New York, Philosophical Library, 1944. Defines thousands of sociological terms. Brief articles, signed with initials.

Social Work Year Book, ed. by R. H. Kurtz. New York, National Association of Social Workers, 1929–date. Pt. 1—Topical articles signed by specialists, bibliographies; Pt. 2—Directories, and an index to both parts. A description of organized activities in social work and in related fields.

Protestant-Catholic-Jew; An Essay in American Religious Sociology, by Will Herberg. New York, Doubleday, 1956. A study of one aspect of the religious situation in the United States from the sociological standpoint to provide a better understanding of both religion and society in mid-twentieth-century America. Bibliographies at ends of chapters. In back, bibliography of chief sources and a full index.

Education

Encyclopedia of Educational Research, ed. by W. S. Monroe. Rev. ed. New York, Macmillan, 1950. Brings together to 1950, evaluates, and interprets studies in the educational field. Excellent bibliographies.

Encyclopedia of Modern Education, ed. by H. H. Rivlin and Herbert Schueler. New York, Philosophical Library, 1943. Offers clear, concise explanations of the basic terms, ideas, and movements in modern education, with emphasis on educational theory and practice in the United States. Contains extensive cross references, and is useful to supplement the *Cyclopedia of Education*, 1913.

For materials more recent than the above works, use the *Education Index*, (see p. 32).

Dictionary of Education, by John Dewey, ed. by R. B. Winn. New York, Philosophical Library, 1959. Comprehensive dictionary of professional terms in education. Alphabetical, with cross references. In the back are alphabetical lists of terms and definitions for education in Canada, England, France, Germany, and Italy.

MAKING
A BIBLIOGRAPHY

A bibliography is a list of books, magazine articles, or other printed materials. Many professors require you to submit with your term papers a list of the books or other sources from which you used information. Other professors check your bibliography before you write the paper to make sure that you have consulted proper sources and used the best material. In any case, you cannot escape experience with bibliographies.

An *author bibliography* is a list of an author's works. A *subject bibliography* is a list of references on a subject. Either may be *complete* or *selective*. If complete, it includes *all* references by an author or on a subject and may be so extensive that it fills a whole book (see pp. 39–46). If selective, it includes only *some* of the possible references, depending upon the purpose for which it is compiled. For instance, a bibliography on the Dead Sea Scrolls for a research scholar differs entirely from one on the same subject for a college freshman, each being selective. Bibliographies with descriptive notes about each book, article, or other entries are called *annotated* bibliographies. The bibliography for a term paper, thesis, or dissertation includes all of the sources from which material was gathered.

To help you choose a subject for a paper or for a bibliography, read an article on the subject in an encyclopedia or other reference book. After this survey gives you the *scope* of the subject, you will have a better idea of where to search for information. Frequently the bibliographies at the ends of such articles suggest excellent sources of material. Taking down full bibliographical information when searching for information saves time in the long run, especially when you have decided what you will use. It prevents having to look up material all over again just to get the paging, the exact title of the book, or the author's full name. It is annoying to be far from the library with everything completely prepared except a few of these essentials, which you failed to copy through negligence or haste.

There are a number of "correct" bibliographical forms, differing slightly even within the realm of acceptability in one graduate school. Some professors are inclined to prefer the form used for their own theses or dissertations. The form given below is adequate and acceptable for both graduate and undergraduate purposes in many institutions of higher learning. An alternate form for references from periodicals is shown, which can be used if a simple form is not desired.

For further investigation of bibliographical form, the following list of books may be useful.

Bowers, Fredson. *Principles of Bibliographical Description*. Princeton, N. J., Princeton University Press, c1949.

Chicago University Press. *A Manual of Style*. Chicago, University of Chicago Press, c1949.

Higgins, M. V. *Bibliography; A Beginner's Guide to the Making, Evaluation and Use of Bibliographies*. New York, Wilson, 1941.

Hook, Lucyle, and M. V. Gaver. *The Research Paper*. 3rd ed. Englewood Cliffs, N. J., Prentice-Hall, c1962.

Hurt, Peyton. *Bibliography and Footnotes; A Style Manual for College and University Students*. Rev. and enl. by M. L. H. Richmond. Berkeley, Calif., University of California Press, c1949.

Parker, W. R., comp. *The MLA Style Sheet*. Rev. ed. New York, Modern Language Assn. of America, c1951.

Witmer, E. M., and E. M. Feagley. *Beginner's Guide to Bibliography*. New York, Teachers College Library, Columbia University, 1935.

For information on thesis writing, the following are useful:

Campbell, W. G. *Form and Style in Thesis Writing*. Boston, Houghton, 1954.

Turabian, K. L. *A Manual for Writers of Term Papers, Theses, and Dissertations*. Chicago, University of Chicago Press, 1960.

You should include the following items, in the order stated:

I. *For Books:*

(1) The name of the author, last name first, (2) the title of the book as it appears on the title page, (3) the edition, if other than the first, (4) the number of volumes in the set if the whole set is used; if a single book, volume is not given, (5) the place of publication, (6) the name of the publisher, (7) the date of publication, and (8) the total paging of the book *if required by your instructor.*

If the author has one given name, write it in full; if more than one, write his initials. If a book has two or three authors, invert only the first author's name, for alphabetical purposes in the bibliography. Place the first line of each entry in "hanging indention": Begin it about four spaces to the *left* of the following lines in that entry. Capitalize the title of the book (with the exception of the articles *a, the, an,* and prepositions, unless one appears as the first word in the title), and underline each word separately. If no date of publication or of copyright is given in the book, indicate that fact by *n.d.* (No place of publication and no publisher are indicated by *n.p.*). If more than one place of publication is listed, give only the first; the name of the city is sufficient except in cases of possible confusion.

PUNCTUATION

Place a period between the author's name and the title of the book; and another period after the title unless the book is edited, translated, illustrated, or the like—in that case, a comma. A colon goes after the place of publication; a comma between the publisher and the date. A period is placed after the date and at the end of the reference if other items are given.

ARRANGEMENT

Books are usually arranged alphabetically according to the last name of the author. If the author's name is not known, place the book alphabetically by the title. Books *edited* by two or three persons may be alphabetized by the name of the editor *or* by the title; those edited by more than three persons must be alphabetized by the title.

ABBREVIATIONS

comp. —compiler, compiled
c   —copyright
ed.   —edition, editor, edited
enl. —enlarged
il.   —illustrated, illustrator
introd.—introduction
n.d. —no date
n.p. —no place of publication

p.   —page
pp.   —pages
pref. —preface
pseud.—pseudonym
rev. —revised
tr.   —translated, translator
vol. —volume
vols. —volumes

Examples:

A. Books by One Author:

Sayers, D. L. The Man Born To Be King; A Play-Cycle on the Life of Our Lord and Saviour, Jesus Christ, Written for Broadcasting. London: V. Gollancz, 1943.

CLIFTON E. OLMSTEAD
Professor of Religion, The George Washington University

History of Religion

in the

United States

PRENTICE-HALL, INC., ENGLEWOOD CLIFFS, N.J.

Olmstead, C. E. History of Religion in the United States. Englewood
Cliffs, N. J.: Prentice-Hall, c1960.

C. FitzSimons Allison

FEAR,
LOVE,
and

WORSHIP

GREENWICH · CONNECTICUT

Allison, C. F. Fear, Love, and Worship. Greenwich, Conn.: The Seabury
Press, c1962.

B. Books by Two or Three Authors:

Price, I. M., O. R. Sellers, and E. L. Carlson. The Monuments and the Old Testament; Light from the Near East on Scriptures. Philadelphia: Judson Press [1958].

C. An Edited Text:

1. *An author's works edited by someone else:*

Calvin, Jean. Institutes of the Christian Religion, ed. by J. T. McNeill, tr. by F. L. Battles. 2 vols. Philadelphia: Westminster Press [c1960].

2. *A collection of different authors' works, edited by one person:*

Anderson, G. H., ed. The Theology of the Christian Mission. New York: McGraw-Hill [c1961].

3. *Books edited by two or three persons, listed by editors or by title:*

Kegley, C. W., and R. W. Bretall, eds. The Theology of Paul Tillich. New York: Macmillan, 1952.

The Theology of Paul Tillich, ed. by C. W. Kegley and R. W. Bretall. New York: Macmillan, 1952.

4. *Books edited by more than three persons:*

A Catholic Commentary on Holy Scripture, ed. by Bernard Orchard, E. F. Subcliffe, and others. New York: Thomas Nelson & Sons [c1953].

D. A Translation or an Illustrated Edition:

Balthasar, H. U. V. Prayer, tr. by A. V. Littledale. New York: Sheed & Ward [c1961].

II. *Corporate Entries* (See p. 12.)

(1) The name of the author of the publication—a person, department, bureau, or organization, (2) the name of the document of publication, (3) the edition, if other than the first, (4) place of publication, (5) the publisher—not abbreviated, and (6) the date of publication.

If the author or editor of a government publication is a *person*, the name of the department or bureau and the number of the bulletin come after the date of publication, in parentheses.

Examples:

U. S. Bureau of the Census. Religious Bodies: 1936. 3 vols. Washington: Government Printing Office, 1941.

Society for Old Testament Study. Eleven Years of Bible Bibliography; The Book Lists of the Society for Old Testament Study, 1946–1956, ed. by H. H. Rowley. Indian Hills, Colo.: Falcon's Wing Press [c1957].

III. *For Articles from Encyclopedias and Other General Reference Books:*

(1) The name of the author of the article, if known, (2) the name of the article as it appears in the book, (3) the name of the book in which the article appears, (4) the edition, if other than the first, or the date of publication, or the copyright date, (5) the volume number, if one of a set of books, and (6) the inclusive paging of the article.

The first line of each entry is placed in "hanging indention." The name of the article is inclosed in quotation marks; the name of the book is underlined, each word separately. Both are capitalized, except articles and prepositions within the title of the book. A period goes after the author's name; a comma between each of the other items of the entry.

Examples:

A. Encyclopedias:

"Theocracy," A Religious Encyclopedia; Or Dictionary of Biblical, Historical, Doctrinal, and Practical Theology, c1883, vol. 3, pp. 2323–2324.

Mabbot, J. D. "Ethics, History of—Modern Ethics," Encyclopaedia Britannica, c1959, vol. 8, pp. 769–778.

B. Yearbooks:

Dennis, W. V. "The Acute Shortage of Clergy," The Episcopal Church Annual, c1961, pp. 9–11.

C. Biographical Dictionaries:

Gordon, Alexander. "Wesley, John," Dictionary of National Biography, c1899, vol. 20, pp. 1214–1225.

"Blake, Eugene Carson," Who's Who in America, 1958–1959, c1958, p. 256.

D. Books of Quotations:

Instead of the name of the "article," give the first line of the quotation, followed by three dots (. . .) if necessary to denote incompleteness.

Old Testament: Deuteronomy 4:6, "Surely this great nation is a wise and understanding people," Home Book of Bible Quotations, c1949, p. 490:3.

IV. *For Articles from Periodicals:*

A. MAGAZINE ARTICLES:

(1) The name of the author of the article, if known, (2) the name of the article, (3) the name of the magazine in which the article appears, (4) the volume

of the magazine, (5) the date, and (6) the inclusive paging of the article.

The first line of each entry is placed in "hanging idention." The volume number of the magazine is given in Arabic numerals; complete numerals are given for the inclusive paging.

PUNCTUATION

Put a period after the author's name. The name of the article is capitalized (except *a, the, an,* and prepositions unless the first word in the title) and inclosed in quotation marks. A comma goes between the name of the article and the name of the magazine. Capitalize the name of the magazine and underline each word separately. A comma goes between the name of the magazine and the volume (abbreviated) number, but no comma between volume and date, which is inclosed in parentheses. If it is a monthly magazine, no comma between month and year. Comma between date and paging; period at end of reference. The month may be written in full or listed in the correct abbreviation, but the selected form must be consistent in a bibliography.

Some magazines are published quarterly and continuously paged throughout the four issues; others are paged separately in each quarterly issue. Also, some are numbered 1, 2, 3, 4, while other quarterly magazines use Spring, Summer, Fall, or Winter to identify issues. *If the paging is not continuous,* either the season or the number of the issue must appear in place of the *month* in the date.

ARRANGEMENT

Articles and stories from magazines and collections are arranged alphabetically according to the author's last name, if known; otherwise, they are arranged by titles.

Examples:

Alexander, G. M. "The Strange Episcopate of Dr. Luscombe," Anglican Theological Review, vol. 41 (October 1959), pp. 286–298.

"Nuclear Power and Christian Faith," Christian Century, vol. 79 (January 31, 1962), pp. 134–135.

ALTERNATE FORM FOR PERIODICAL REFERENCES

The difference between the above and the following forms are in the volume and date indications. Many scholarly researchers use the following form, even though many students and even library workers have difficulty in reading Roman numerals and in transposing them to and from Arabic numerals. In this form only the *year* is given for journals and other periodicals which are published quarterly. Use capital Roman numerals for volume. Do not use *p.* or *pp.* for paging.

Examples:

Alexander, G. M. "The Strange Episcopate of Dr. Luscombe," Anglican Theological Review, XLI (October 1959), 286–298.

"Nuclear Power and Christian Faith," Christian Century, LXXIX (January 31, 1962), 134–135.

B. NEWSPAPER ARTICLES:

Newspaper article references have the same form as magazine article references, except that a newspaper reference cites the *page* and *column* and occasionally the *section*. There is no volume. (See p. 32.)

Examples:

Peck, Marion, "Dose of Compassion Best Remedy for Alcoholism, Ministers Told," Chattanooga Daily Times, (February 3, 1962), p. 1, col. 6.

"J.B., by A. MacLeish: Comments on Play," New York Times, (December 7, 1958), sec. 2, p. 5, col. 5.

Sample Bibliography:

Samaria in the Light of Archaeological Research

A Bibliography

Books

Albright, W. F. Archaeology and the Religion of Israel. Baltimore: Johns Hopkins Press, 1942.

———, "The Biblical Period," The Jews: Their History, Culture and Religion, c1949, vol. 1, pp. 3–69.

Finegan, Jack. Light from the Ancient Past; The Archaeological Background of Judaism and Christianity. 2nd ed. Princeton, N. J.: Princeton University Press, 1959.

Jack, J. W. Samaria in Ahab's Time; Harvard Excavations and Their Results, with Chapters on the Political and Religious Situation. Edinburgh: T. & T. Clark, 1929.

Parrot, Andre. Samaria; The Capitol of the Kingdom of Israel. London: S.C.M. Press [c1958].

Pritchard, J. B., ed. Ancient Near Eastern Texts Relating to the Old Testament. 2nd ed. Princeton, N. J.: Princeton University Press, 1955.

Reisner, G. A., C. S. Fisher, and D. G. Lyon. Harvard Excavations at Samaria, 1908–1910. Cambridge, Mass.: Harvard University Press, 1924.

Robertson, Edward. "Samaria," Encyclopaedia Britannica, c1961, vol, 19, p. 918.

Seligsohn, Max. "Samaria," Jewish Encyclopedia, c1916, vol. 10, pp. 667–669.

The Westminster Historical Atlas to the Bible, ed. by G. E. Wright, F. V. Filson, and W. F. Albright. Philadelphia: Westminster Press, 1956.

Periodicals

Bowman, John. "Early Samaritan Eschatology," Journal of Jewish Studies, vol. 6, no. 2 (1955), pp. 63–72.

"Harvard Expedition Resumes Excavations on Site of Samaria," New York Times, (April 12, 1931), p. 30, col. 5.

Reed, W. L., and G. L. Harding. "Archaeological News from Jordan," The Biblical Archaeologist, vol. 16 (February 1953), pp. 2–17.

Wright, G. E., "Archaeology and Old Testament Studies," Journal of Biblical Literature, vol. 77 (March 1958), pp. 39–51.

TITLE
AND SUBJECT
INDEX

A

Abbreviations:
  explained in dictionaries, 50
  found in card catalog, 9, 12
  in bibliographies, 102
  in periodical indexes, 24
  in reference books, 19, 34
Abingdon Bible Commentary, 72
Abstracting tools, theological, 37–38
Abstracts:
  history, 89
  psychology, 33, 37
  theology, 37–38
Addenda, 50
Aftermath, 86
Album of American History, 89
Allgemeine Deutsche Biographie, 81
*An Alphabetical Subject Index and Index
  Encyclopaedia to Periodical Articles
  on Religion, 1890–1899*, 29
Alphabetizing:
  bibliographies, 102, 107
  card catalog, 9–10
  encyclopedias, 52
  letter by letter, 70
  magazine articles, 23
  periodical indexes, 23
  reference books, 19
  word by word, 9–10
Ambassador World Atlas, 90
American Authors and Books, 1640–1940,
  95
American Authors, 1600–1900, 82
The American Book of Days, 88

The American Catholic Who's Who, 78–79
American Christianity . . . , 85
American-English Usage, 96
*The American Historical Association's
  Guide to Historical Literature*, 35,
  42
American Jewish Yearbook, 61
American Missionaries in China, 45
American Synagogue Directory, 63
American Yearbook, 64
Americana Annual, 56, 63
Americana Encyclopedia, 52, 56, 63
Anabaptist-Mennonite Movement, 55
Analytical Concordance to the Bible, 72–
  73
Analytics, in card catalog, 14
The Ancestry of Our English Bible . . . , 67
*Ancient Christian Writers; The Works of
  the Fathers in Translation*, 92
Annotated bibliography, 100
Annual Register of World Events, 64
Anonymous literature, 94–95
*Ante-Nicene Fathers; Translation of the
  Writings of the Fathers Down to
  A.D. 325*, 92
Antonyms:
  book of, 96
  in dictionaries, 50
Arrangement:
  bibliographies, 102, 107
  books on shelves, 2
  cards in catalog, 8–10
  encyclopedias, 52
  periodical indexes, 23
  reference books, 19

Art Index, 32–33
Articles, *the, a, an:*
    at beginning of title on catalog cards, 9,
        12
    within title in bibliographies, 102, 107
Atlas of American History, 89–90
Atlas of the Bible, 74
Atlas of the Classical World, 74
Atlas of the Early Christian World, 74
Atlas of World History, 89
Atlases:
    Bible, 74
    general, 89–91
Author analytics, 14
Author bibliography, 100
Author cards in catalog, 9, 11
Author entries in bibliographies, 101–102,
        105–107
Author numbers, 5

B

Baker's Dictionary of Theology, 47
A Baptist Bibliography, 41
The Baptist Encyclopedia, 54
The Baptist Handbook, 62
A Basic Bibliography for Ministers, 41
Beginner's Guide to Bibliography, 101
*The Best American Short Stories . . . and
        the Yearbook of the American Short
        Story,* 96
The Best Plays of . . . , 96
Bible, 67–74
    atlases, 74
    commentaries, 71–72
    companions to, 70–71
    concordances, 72–73
    dictionaries, 69–71
    editions, 42–43, 67
    encyclopedias, 69
    quotations, 93
    reference tools for study, 67–68
    translations, 67
    versions, 67
The Bible Companion . . . , 71
Biblia Hebraica, 68
Biblical language:
    dictionaries, 51, 68, 93–94
    grammars, 68–69
Biblical Subject Index, 29, 73
Bibliographi Historiae Philosophiae, 42
Bibliographia Ad Usum Seminarioum, 40
Bibliographia Philosophica, 1934–1945, 42
Bibliographic Index . . . , 30, 41
Bibliographical form, 100–109
*A Bibliographical Guide to the History of
        Christianity,* 44
Bibliographies:
    annotated, 100

Bibliographies *(Cont.)*
    author, 100
    complete, 100
    definitions of kinds, 100
    directions for compiling, 100–109
    in reference books, 19
    sample, 108–109
    selective, 100
    subject, 100
    theological, 39–46
Bibliography, *see* Bibliographies
Bibliography; A Beginner's Guide . . . ,
        101
Bibliography and Footnotes . . . , 101
Bibliography of American Literature, 42
*A Bibliography of Bible Study for Theo-
        logical Students,* 44
*A Bibliography of Bibliographies in Re-
        ligion,* 39–40
*A Bibliography of Post-Graduate Masters'
        Theses in Religion,* 46
A Bibliography of Practical Theology, 41
*A Bibliography of Systematic Theology for
        Theological Students,* 41
*Bibliography of the Continental Reforma-
        tion . . . ,* 45–46
*Bibliography of the Theology of Missions
        in the Twentieth Century,* 45
Bibliotheca Missionum, 45
Bibliotheca Symbolica Universalis . . . , 83
Biographical Encyclopedia of the World,
        80
Biography:
    general, 79–82
    index to, 34
    theological, 77–79
Biography Index, 34
Black's Bible Dictionary, 69
*. . . The Book Lists of the Society for Old
        Testament Study, 1946–1956,* 43
Book numbers, 4–5
The Book of Catholic Quotations, 93
Book Review Digest, 34
Book reviews:
    indexes to, 34
    listed in periodical indexes, 28, 34
Bookman's Manual, 67
Britannica Book of the Year, 56, 63
Britannica Encyclopaedia, 52, 56, 63
British Humanities Index, 36
Bulletin of Bibliography, 34
Butler's The Lives of the Saints, 78

C

Call numbers, 4–5, 17
The Cambridge Ancient History, 88
Cambridge History of American Literature,
        95

Cambridge History of English Literature, 94
The Cambridge Mediaeval History, 88
The Cambridge Modern History, 88
Canon law, 40, 67
Card catalog, 8–17
    arrangement, 9–10
    as index to book collection, 8, 23
    details on cards, 10–11
Care of books, 20
Cassell's Encyclopedia of World Literature, 96
Catalog, card, see Card catalog
Catholic Authors, 82
Catholic Biblical Encyclopedia (Old and New Testament), 69
The Catholic Bookman's Guide . . . , 40–41
The Catholic Church in America; An Historical Bibliography, 44
A Catholic Commentary on Holy Scripture, 72
A Catholic Dictionary (The Catholic Encyclopaedia Dictionary), 48
The Catholic Directory, 62
Catholic Encyclopedia, 53
Catholic literature, indexes to, 28–29
Catholic Periodical Index, 23, 28
Catholic periodicals, indexes to, 40–41
Catholic Periodicals of Theological Interest, 41
The Catholic Who's Who, 79
Caxton World Atlas, 90
Century Cyclopedia of Names, 91
Chambers's Biographical Dictionary, 80
Chambers's Encyclopaedia, 57, 80
The Christian Annual, 60
Christian Periodical Index, 29
Christianity in a Revolutionary Age, 85
Christianity in Japan; A Bibliography of Japanese and Chinese Sources, 45
"The Church Fathers," 92
The Church of Scotland Year-Book, 60
Churches and Church Membership in the United States . . . , 61
Class numbers, 4, 5
Classic Myths in English Literature and in Art . . . , 87
Classification of books, 2–7
    Dewey Decimal Classification, 2, 3–4
    Library of Congress Classification, 2, 5–7
    Union Theological Seminary Classification, 2, 7
The Clerical Directory of the Protestant Episcopal Church in the U. S. of A., 62
Collier's Encyclopedia, 57
Collier's Encyclopedia Year Book, 57, 64

Columbia Dictionary of Modern European Literature, 95
Columbia Encyclopedia, 91
Columbia Lippincott Gazetteer of the World, 90
Commentaries, 71–72
Commercial Atlas and Marketing Guide, 90
A Companion to the Bible, 70
Complete Concordance to the Bible (Douay Version), 73
A Complete Concordance to the Holy Scriptures . . . , 73
Concise Bible Commentary, 72
A Concise Dictionary of Ecclesiastical Terms, 48
Concise Dictionary of Judaism, 48
The Concise Encyclopaedia of Living Faiths, 53
The Concise Encyclopaedia of Western Philosophy and Philosophers, 97–98
Concordance to the Bible (Douay Version), 73
Concordances, 72–73
Congressional Quarterly Almanac, 65
The Congressional Year Book, 60
Conspectus of American Biography, 81
Copyright date, 19
Corporate entries:
    card catalog, 12
    in bibliographies, 105
Corpus Christianorum, 92
Cosmopolitan World Atlas, 90
. . . The Creeds of Christendom . . . , 83
Critical Bibliography of Biblical Literature, 40
Critical Bibliography of Canon Law, 40
Critical Bibliography of Empirical Psychology, 40
Critical Bibliography of Liturgical Literature, 40
Critical Bibliography of Missiology, 40
A Critical Bibliography of Religion in America, 44, 86
Critical Bibliography of Sociology, 40
Crockford's Clerical Directory, 62–63
Cross references:
    in card catalog, 9, 12, 15–16
    in indexes, 24, 28
    in periodical indexes, 24
    in reference books, 19, 20
    name, 16
Cumulation, 23
Cumulative Book Index, 34
Curiosities of Popular Customs and of Rites, Ceremonies, Observances, and Miscellaneous Antiquities, 87
Current Biography, Who's News and Why, 80
Current Biography Yearbook, 80

Cyclopedia of Education, 99
Cyclopedia of Methodism, 55

D

Date:
in bibliographical references, 101, 105, 107
of reference books, 18–19
of yearbooks, 59
on catalog card, 11
Days and Customs of All Faiths, 87–88
Decimal classification, 2–4
Dewey classification, 2–4
Dewey Decimal Classification, 2–4
Dictionaries:
Bible, 69–70
Bible study, 69–71
Biblical language, 68–69
foreign language, 50–51, 68
general, 49–50
mythology, 87
sociology, 99
theology, 47–49
Dictionary and Thesaurus of the Hebrew Language, 68
Dictionary of All Scriptures and Myths, 47
Dictionary of American Biography, 81
A Dictionary of American-English Usage, 96
Dictionary of American History, 89, 90
Dictionary of American Hymnology, 49
Dictionary of Anonymous and Pseudonymous English Literature, 94–95
Dictionary of Catholic Biography, 78
Dictionary of Christ and the Gospels, 70
Dictionary of Christian Antiquities, 77
A Dictionary of Christian Biography and Literature to the End of the Sixth Century A.D. . . . , 77–78
A Dictionary of Christian Biography, Literature, Sects, and Doctrines . . . , 77
Dictionary of Education, 99
A Dictionary of English Church History, 47
Dictionary of European History, 89
A Dictionary of Hymnology . . . , 48–49
A Dictionary of Life in Bible Times, 69–70
Dictionary of Mysticism, 87
Dictionary of Mythology, Folklore and Symbols, 87
Dictionary of National Biography, 80
Dictionary of Papal Pronouncements, Leo XIII to Pius XII, 48
A Dictionary of Pastoral Psychology, 98
Dictionary of Philosophy and Psychology, 98

Dictionary of Philosophy in the Words of Philosophers, 98
Dictionary of Scholastic Philosophy, 98
Dictionary of Social Science, 99
Dictionary of Sociology, 99
A Dictionary of the Bible, 70
Dictionary of the Popes, from Peter to Pius XII, 79
Dictionary of Universal Biography of All Ages and All Peoples, 80
Dictionary of World Literature, 96
Directories, theological, 62–63
Directory of American Scholars, 82
Directory of Newspapers and Periodicals, 90–91
Directory of World Missions, 63
Dissertation, writing, 101
Doctoral Dissertations in the Field of Religion, 1940–1952, 46
Doctoral Dissertations in the Field of Religion, 1952–1961, . . . , 46
Doctrines, 84
Documents Illustrative of the History of the Church, 83
Documents of the Christian Church, 83–84
Dogma, history of, 84
Drama, indexes to, 34–35
Dramatic Index, 34
Dutch-English, English-Dutch Dictionary, 51

E

Ecclesiastical terms, 48
Editions:
filed in card catalog, 10
in bibliographical references, 101, 105, 106
of atlases, 90
of reference books, 18
on catalog cards, 11
Editor, in bibliographical references, 105
Education:
dictionary of, 99
encyclopedias of, 99
index to, 32–33
Education Index, 32–33, 99
The Eleven Religions and Their Proverbial Lore, 84
Enchiridion Symbolorum, 84
Enciclopedia Cattolica, 54
Enciclopedia Filosofica, 97
Enciclopedia Italiana di Scienze ed Arti, 57
Encyclopaedia Biblica . . . , 69
Encyclopaedia Britannica, 52, 56
Enclodaedia Britannica World Atlas, 90
Encyclopaedia Judiaca, 56
The Encyclopaedia of Islam, 56

Encyclopaedia of Religion and Religions, 53

Encyclopaedia of the Presbyterian Church in the United States of America . . . , 55

Encyclopaedia of the Social Sciences, 98

Encyclopedia Americana, 52, 56

Encyclopedia of American History, 89

Encyclopedia of Bible Life, 69

Encyclopedia of Biblical Interpretation, A Millennial Anthology, 69

Encyclopedia of Educational Research, 99

The Encyclopedia of Jewish Knowledge, 55

An Encyclopedia of Latin-American History, 89

Encyclopedia of Literature, 96

Encyclopedia of Modern Education, 99

An Encyclopedia of Religion, 53

Encyclopedia of Religion and Ethics, 52

Encyclopedia of Religious Knowledge, 53

Encyclopedia of Southern Baptists, 54

Encyclopedia of World History, 88–89

Encyclopedia of World Literature, 96

Encyclopedia supplements, 59, 63–64

Encyclopedias:
  Bible, 69
  general, 56–57
  theological, 52–56

The English Bible in America . . . , 43, 67

English literature, 94–95

English usage, 96

The Episcopal Church Annual, 60

Essay and General Literature Index, 35

Essential Books for a Pastor's Study; Basic and Recommended Works, 41

Europa; The Encyclopedia of Europe, 64

Europa Year Book, 64

European literature, 94–95

Evangelical and Reformed Hymnal, 62

Everyman's Dictionary of Non-Classical Mythology, 87

The Exhaustive Concordance of the Bible, 73

F

Familiar Quotations, 96

"The Fathers of the Church," 92

The Fathers of the Church; A New Translation, 93

Federal Council Yearbook, 60

Fiction:
  historical, 35
  guides to, 35

Fiction Index, 36

Filing code for card catalog, 9–10, 14, 15, 16

Folklore, 87

Footnotes, instructions for, 101

Foreign articles at beginning of title, filed in card catalog, 9, 12

Foreign-language dictionaries, 50–51

Foreign-language grammars, 68, 69

Foreign words, in dictionaries, 50

Form and Style in Thesis Writing, 101

FPA Book of Quotations, 96

Funk and Wagnalls New Standard Dictionary, 50

Funk and Wagnalls Standard Dictionary of Folklore, Mythology and Legend, 87

Funk and Wagnalls Standard Handbook of Synonyms, Antonyms and Prepositions, 96

G

Gazetteers, 50, 90

Geography, *see* Atlases

Glossaries, 56

The Golden Bough; A Study in Magic and Religion, 86

Government:
  as author, 12
  publications, 65

A Grammar of the Greek New Testament in the Light of Historical Research, 69

Grammar of the Hebrew Language, 68

Grammars, foreign-language, 68, 69

Grand Larousse Encyclopédique, 57

Granger's Index to Poetry, 36

A Greek-English Lexicon, 68

A Greek-English Lexicon of the New Testament, 68

A Greek-English Lexicon of the New Testament and Other Early Christian Literature, 68

Grollenberg's Atlas of the Bible, 74

Die Grosen Biographie, Deutsche Biographie, 81–82

Der Grosse Brockhaus, 57

Guide cards, in card catalog, 9

Guide to American Catholic History, 44–45

Guide to Catholic Literature, 28–29, 40

Guide to Historical Fiction, 35

Guide to Historical Literature, 35

Guide to the Best Fiction, 35

Guide to the Best Historical Novels and Tales, 35

H

Hammond's Ambassador World Atlas, 90

Hammond's Standard World Atlas, 90

Hammond's Universal World Atlas, 90

The Handbook of Biblical Personalities, 78
Handbook of Denominations in the United States, 61
Handbook of Universal History, 89
Handbook to Literature, 96
Handbooks, theological, 61–62
Harper's Bible Dictionary, 69
Harper's Latin Dictionary, 50
Harper's Standard French and English Dictionary, 51
Harper's Topical Concordance, 73
A Hebrew and English Lexicon of the Old Testament, 68
Historic Notebook, 89
Historical Abstracts, 1775–1945, 89
Historical Atlas, 89
Historical Atlas of the Holy Land, 74
Historical Atlas of the United States, 90
Historical Atlas to the Bible, 74
Historical Catalogue of the Printed Editions of Holy Scripture in the Library of the British and Foreign Bible Society, 42–43, 67
Historical fiction, *see* Fiction, historical
Historical Statistics of the United States, Colonial Times to 1957, 65
Historical Statistics of the United States, 1789–1945, 65
Historical Statistics of the United States, 1946–1952, 65
History:
  general, 88–89
  theological, 83–88
A History of Christianity, 85
History of Dogma, 84
A History of Philosophy, 97
History of Religion in the United States, 85–86
A History of the Expansion of Christianity, 84–85
History of the Jews, 86
Home Book of Bible Quotations, 93
Home Book of Modern Verse, 96
Home Book of Quotations, 96
Home Book of Verse, 96
How Our Bible Came to Us: Its Texts and Versions, 67
The Hymnal 1940 Companion, 62
Hymnology, 48, 62
Hyphenated words, in card catalog, 10

I

Identical names, filed in card catalog, 10
Illustrations, listed on catalog card, 11
Illustrator:
  in bibliographical references, 102, 105
  on catalog card, 11
Imprint, 11

Index:
  abbreviations in, 24, 32
  arrangement of, 23
  cross references in, 24, 27
  in atlases, 89–91
  in books, 19
  in encyclopedias, 52
  to magazines, 23–36
  to newspapers, 32
  to periodicals, 23–36
  to plays, 34–35
  to poems, 36
  to short stories, 35–36
Index Islamicus, 1906–1955, 29
Index to Full Length Plays, 35
Index to One-Act Plays, 35
Index to Plays, 34–35
Index to Plays in Collections, 35
Index to Poetry, 36
Index to Poetry and Recitations, 36
Index to Religious Periodical Literature, 23, 24–27, 29
Index to Short Stories, 35
Information Please Almanac, 64
Initials:
  in bibliographical references, 101–102
  in filing, 13
Institutional publications, 12
International Bibliography of the History of Religion for the Year, 40
International Critical Commentary, 71
International Index . . . , 30
International Index to Periodicals, 30
International Review of Biblical Studies, 38
International Standard Bible Encyclopedia, 69
International Who's Who, 80
International World Atlas, 90
International Year Book and Statesmen's Who's Who, 65
Internationale Zeitschriftenschau für Bibelwissenschaft und Grenzgebiete, 38
The Interpreter's Bible . . . , 71–72
The Interpreter's Dictionary of the Bible, 70
An Introductory Bibliography for the Study of Scripture, 43–44, 68
Inverted subject headings, *see* Subject headings, inverted
Italian-English, English-Italian Dictionary, 51

J

Jewish Encyclopedia, 55
Jewish Symbols in the Greco-Roman Period, 86

Joint author:
    card in catalog, 12
    in bibliographical references, 105

L

Labels on card catalog trays, 9
Larned, *see New Larned History*
Leaders in Education, 82
Letter-by-letter alphabetizing, 10, 52
Lexicon in Veteris Testamenti Libros, 68
Lexicons, 68
Library of Christian Classics, 93
Library of Congress:
    catalog cards, 8
    classification, 2, 5–6
Library of the World's Best Literature, 96
Life Pictorial Atlas of the World, 90
Literary History of England, 94
Literary History of the United States, 95
Literature, 92–96
    general, 94–96
    index to, 35
    theological, 92–94
Liturgical dictionary, 48
Liturgical literature, bibliography of, 40
The Lives of the Saints, 78
Livres Catholiques, 40
Lutheran Cyclopedia, 54
Lutterworth Topical Concordance, 73

M

McKay's Modern English-Norwegian and Norwegian-English Dictionary, 51
McKay's Modern Danish-English, English-Danish Dictionary, 51
Magazine articles:
    in bibliographical references, 106–08
    indexes to, 23–36
Magazine indexes, *see* Periodical indexes
Magazine Subject Index, 34
Main entry card, in card catalog, 10
A Manual for Writers of Term Papers, Theses, and Dissertations, 101
A Manual Grammar of the Greek New Testament, 68
A Manual of Style, 101
Maps, use of index in atlases, 89–91
Masterpieces of World Philosophy, in Summary Form, 97
The Mennonite Encyclopedia . . . , 55
Methodist Bishops . . . , 79
The Methodist Periodical Index, 29
"Migne," 92
Ministerial Dictionary of the Presbyterian Church, 63

Missiology, 40
The MLA Style Sheet, 101
Modern English Usage, 96
Multipurpose Tools for Bible Study, 43, 68
Music Index, 36
Mythological characters, biography of, 80
Mythology, 42, 47, 80, 86–87
Mythology of All Races, 86
Mythology; The Age of Fable; The Age of Chivalry; Legends of Charlemagne, 86

N

"Name" cross references, 16
The National Catholic Almanac, 60
Nelson's Complete Concordance to the Revised Standard Version, 73
Neue Deutsche Biographie, 81
The New Bible Commentary, 72
The New Cambridge Modern History, 88
New Catholic Encyclopedia, 53–54
New Century Cyclopedia of Names, 79
New Century Handbook of English Literature, 94
New Cyclopedia of Practical Quotations, 96
New Dictionary of American History, 89
The New Dictionary of Psychology, 98
New English Dictionary, 50
The New Golden Bough, 86
New International Dictionary, 49–50
New International Encyclopaedia, 63
New International Yearbook, 63–64
New Larned History for Ready Reference, . . . , 88
New Schaff-Herzog Encyclopedia of Religious Knowledge, 53
New Standard Dictionary, 50
New Testament Abstracts, 38
New Testament Literature; An Annotated Bibliography, 44
New York Times Index, 32
Newspapers:
    bibliographical form for articles, 108
    directory, 90–91
    index to, 32
. . . Nicene and Post-Nicene Fathers of the Christian Church, 92
1962 Year Book of the Evangelical and Reformed Church, 60
Nineteenth Century Readers' Guide, 30
Numerals:
    in names of religious hierarchy, filing in catalog, 10
    in names of royalty, filing in catalog, 10
    in titles of books, filing in catalog, 12–13

O

The Official Catholic Directory, 62
*The Official Year-Book of the National As-
  sembly of the Church of England*,
  60
One-act plays, index to, 35
Open stacks, 8
Oxford Classical Dictionary, 94
Oxford Companion to American Literature,
  95
Oxford Companion to Classical Literature,
  96
Oxford Companion to English Literature,
  95
Oxford Companion to French Literature,
  96
Oxford Dictionary, 50
Oxford Dictionary of Quotations, 96
*The Oxford Dictionary of the Christian
  Church*, 47
The Oxford English Dictionary . . . , 50
Oxford History of English Literature, 94

P

Pageant of America, 89
Paging:
  in bibliographical references, 101, 106,
    107, 108
  on catalog card, 11
Papal pronouncements, 48
*Patrologiae Curus Completus Seu Bibli-
  otheca Universalis . . . Series Latina 1844–1880 . . . Series Graeca
  1857–1866*, 92
Periodical indexes, 23–36
  arrangement, 23
Periodicals:
  bibliographical form for articles, 106–08
  cards for, in card catalog, 15
  directories of, 36, 90–91
  indexes to, 23–36
  volumes listed on catalog card, 15
Periodicals Directory, 36
Philosophy, 97–98
Pictorial History of Protestantism . . . , 85
Place of publication:
  in bibliographical references, 101, 105
  on catalog card, 11
Play Index, 35
Plays:
  indexed in *Readers' Guide*, 30
  indexes to, 34–35
Ploetz's Epitome of History, 89
Poems:
  index to, 36
  listed in periodical indexes, 28, 30
Poetry, index to, 36

Political Handbook of the World, 65–66
Poole's Index to Periodical Literature, 30
Popes through the Ages, 79
Post-Nicene Fathers, 92
Prentice-Hall's World Atlas, 90
Prepositions, handbook of, 96
Principles of Bibliographical Description,
  101
Pronunciation, symbols in dictionaries, 49,
  50
*Protestant-Catholic-Jew; An Essay in Amer-
  ican Religious Sociology*, 99
A Protestant Dictionary, 48
Pseudonym, 12, 16
Pseudonymous literature, 94–95
Psychological Abstracts, 33, 37
*Psychological Abstracts: Abstract Refer-
  ences*, 33
Psychological Index, 1894–1935, 33
Psychology:
  abstracts, 33, 37
  dictionaries, 96
  index to, 33
Public Affairs Information Service, 33
Publisher:
  in bibliographical references, 101, 102,
    105
  on catalog card, 11
Punctuation, in bibliographical references,
  102, 107

Q

Quotations, 93–96
  Bible, 93
  Catholic, 93
  general, 96
  Jewish, 93

R

Rand McNally Bible Atlas, 74
*Rand McNally Commercial Atlas and Mar-
  keting Guide*, 90
*The Reader's Adviser and Bookman's Man-
  ual*, 67
Reader's Encyclopedia, 96
Reader's Guide to Periodical Literature,
  29–30
Readings in Church History, 84
Reference books:
  arrangement, 19
  authority, 19
  bibliographical form for articles, 106
  bibliographies in, 19
  care of, 20
  cross references in, 20
  date of, 18–19
  explanation, 18–20
  signed articles in, 19

Reference books (*Cont.*)
subjects covered, 19
Religion, encyclopedias of, 52–56
Religion in American Life, 86
Religion in the Twentieth Century, 85
Religion in Twentieth Century America, 85
Religions, Mythologies, Folklore: An An-
notated Bibliography, 42
Religious and Theological Abstracts, 29, 37
Religious Bodies: 1936, 61
The Religious Bodies of America, 61
Religious Leaders in America, 78
The Research Paper, 101
Research Studies in Education, 33

S

"See also" references, *see* Cross references
"See" references, *see* Cross references
A Select Library of Nicene and Post-Nicene
Fathers of the Christian Church, 92
Selective bibliography, 100
Seventh-Day Adventist Bible Commentary,
72
Seventh-Day Adventist Bible Dictionary,
70
Short Dictionary of Mythology, 87
Short stories:
indexes to, 35–36
Yearbook of American, 96
Short Story Index, 35–36
Shorter Atlas of the Bible, 74
Shorter Encyclopaedia of Islam, 56
Signed articles, in reference books, 19
A Small Liturgical Dictionary, 48
Social Sciences:
dictionary of, 99
encyclopedia of, 98
Social Work Year Book, 99
Society publications, 12
Sociology, 98–99
bibliography of, 40
theological, 99
Song Index, 36
Source Book and Bibliographical Guide for
American Church History, 45
Sources Chrétiennes, 93
The Sources of Catholic Dogma, 84
South American Handbook, 65
Spanish and English Dictionary, 51
Speech Index, 36
. . . Standard Dictionary of Folklore, My-
thology and Legend, 87
Standard Handbook of Synonyms, Anto-
nyms and Prepositions, 96
The Standard Jewish Encyclopedia, 55–56
Standard World Atlas, 90
Stateman's Year-Book, 65
Statistical Abstract of the United States, 65

The Story of Our Hymns . . . , 62
Studia Liturgica . . . , 38
Subdivided subject headings, filed in card
catalog, 14
Subject analytics, in card catalog, 14
Subject bibliography, 100
Subject cards in card catalog, 13–14
Subject headings:
in card catalog, 9, 13–14
inverted, 14
phrase, 14
subdivided, 14
Subject Index to Periodicals, 1915–1922;
1926– , 36
Subjects, listed on catalog cards, 11
Symbols:
Jewish, 86
mythology, folklore, 87
Synonymous subjects, in card catalog, 15
Synonyms:
books of, 96
in dictionaries, 49, 50

T

Temporary card, in card catalog, 10
10 Eventful Years, 89
Term paper, writing, 101
The Text, Canon, and Principal Versions of
the Bible . . . , 67
Textbook of the History of Doctrines, 84
Theological dictionaries, 47–49
A Theological German Vocabulary, 51
Theological libraries, 1
A Theological Word Book, 71
Theologische Literarzeitung, 38
Theologisches Wörterbuch zum Neuen
Testament, 68
Thesis, writing, 101
Third New International Dictionary, 49–50
Times Atlas of the World, 90
Title card, in card catalog, 12–13
Title entries in *Readers' Guide*, 30
Tools for Bible Study, 43, 68
Translator, in bibliographical references,
105
A Treasury of Jewish Quotations, 93
Twentieth Century Authors, 82
The Twentieth Century Bible Commen-
tary, 71
Twentieth Century Encyclopedia of Cathol-
icism, 54
Twentieth Century Encyclopedia of Reli-
gious Knowledge, 53

U

Ulrich's Periodicals Directory, 36
Union Theological Seminary Classification,
2, 6–7

United Church of Christ . . . Year Book, 60
United Nations publications, 66
United Nations Statistical Year Book, 66
United States Catalog, 34
United States Government Organization Manual, 65
United States Public Documents:
  card in card catalog, 12
  in bibliographical references, 105
Universal Jewish Encyclopedia, 55
Universal Pronouncing Dictionary of Biography and Mythology, 80
Universal World Atlas, 90

V

Versions of the Bible, 67
Vocabulary of the Bible, 70
The Vocabulary of the Church; A Pronunciation Guide, 93–94
Volumes, number of:
  in bibliographical references, 106, 107
  on catalog card, 11

W

Warner's Library of the World's Best Literature, 96
Webster's Biographical Dictionary, 80
Webster's Dictionary of Synonyms, 96
Webster's Geographical Dictionary, 91
Webster's New International Dictionary, 50
Webster's Third New International Dictionary, 49–50
The Westminster Dictionary of the Bible, 70
Westminster Historical Atlas to the Bible, 74

White's Conspectus of American Biography, 81
Who Was Who, 81
Who Was Who in America, 81
. . . Who's News and Why, 80
Who's Who, 81
Who's Who in America, 81
Who's Who in Methodism, 79
Who's Who in the Bible, 78
Who's Who in the Clergy, 78
Who's Who in the Protestant Clergy, 79
Who's Who in World Jewry . . . , 79
The Wisdom of the Living Religions, 84
Word-by-word alphabetizing, 9–10, 52
World Almanac, 64, 90
World Atlas, 90
A World Bibliography of Bibliographies, 41
World Biography, 80
World Christian Handbook, 61
World literature, 96
World Religions . . . , 83
The World's Great Religions, 83

Y

The Year Book of the Congregational Christian Churches of the United States of America, 60
Year Book of the Evangelical and Reformed Church, 60
Yearbook of American Churches . . . , 59–60
Yearbook of the United Nations, 66
Yearbooks:
  general, 63–65
  theological, 59–61